DEMONS

CARLTON
BOOKS

THIS IS A CARLTON BOOK
This edition published in 2007 by
Carlton Books Limited,
20 Mortimer Street
London
W1T 3JW

Text and design copyright
© Carlton Books Limited.
This books is sold subject to the
condition that it shall not, by way of
trade or otherwise, be lent, resold,
hired out or otherwise circulated

A CIP catalogue record of this book is
available from the British Library.

ISBN: 978 1 84442 098 8

Printed and bound in China

Executive Editor: Lisa Dyer
Senior Art Editor: Zoë Dissell
Designer: Michelle Pickering
Copy Editor: Nicky Gyopari
Picture Researcher: Jenny Lord
Production: Caroline Alberti

Laura Ward and Will Steeds

Contents

Introduction

The Devil, Satan, Lucifer, Beelzebub – these are just some of the many names that have been used to describe the personification of evil in Christian belief over the span of almost 3,000 years that has elapsed since the time of the very earliest biblical writers. The Old Testament itself was written over a period of almost a thousand years, from close to 1,000 BC to – it is thought – nigh on 150 BC. By the dawn of the Christian era and the time of the New Testament writers, the concept of a malevolent supernatural being had been shaped into an arch-personification of evil itself, or the 'Evil One' – a single entity, albeit with a horde of evil spirits, or demons, as its nefarious hangers-on and henchmen.

The 'character' of this powerful but wholly negative spiritual force evolved during the Old Testament period, undergoing a particular transformation during the time of the Apocalyptic Jewish writers (200 BC–100 AD), so called because of their reported revelations of the end of the world. For over this time the Jews were becoming especially preoccupied with the problem of evil; and, under keen oppression during the later period, the emergence of a 'personality' of the Devil, or Satan, reflected a strongly rooted impulse on the part of the Jewish writers – and, crucially, the 'seers' who would generate the books of the so-called Apocrypha – to understand the significance and role of evil in a world ruled over by God.

Apocrypha, or 'hidden books' (in reference to the mysterious nature of their origin) of the Apocalyptic period, together with 'Pseudepigrapha' (so called, because supposedly written by the ancient writers under whose names they appeared) influenced both contemporary authors and the early Christian writers. In the pseudepigraphic Book of Enoch, for example, the sinful *bene ha-elohim* or 'sons of God' from Genesis became, instead, Watcher Angels, earning the epithet because of their prurient interest in mortal women. The Watcher Angels followed a leader called Semyaza and had sexual relations with female humans, prompting the Lord to send a deluge upon the earth. For introducing humankind to wicked ways, the Watcher Angels were cast by avenging archangels into underworld pits of darkness.

The Jewish writers of the Old Testament period were themselves influenced by their Persian neighbours in the region that is now Iran, where the dualistic religion of Zoroastrianism centred on Ahura Mazda, a god of creation, and Angra Mainyu (or Ahriman), a destructive god associated with snakes, demons and all things evil. Also, the prophet Zoroaster had taught that there would be a final reckoning, in which the evil would be dispatched to a hell of flames and ghastly torments.

Other names – Belial, Azazel, Mastema, Satanail, as well as Satan – reduced more often to the single figure of 'the Evil One' during the later Old Testament period and in the apocryphal literature, with Satan becoming the name most closely associated with a single source of evil. Indeed, in a substantive shift Zechariah, in the penultimate book of the Old Testament, describes a definite figure, with 'Joshua the high priest standing before the angel of the Lord, and Satan standing at his right hand to resist him. And the Lord said unto Satan, "The Lord rebuke thee, O Satan"' (Zechariah 3:1–2). The Greek translation of the Hebrew Scriptures (known as the Septuagint translation) in the 3rd and 2nd centuries BC also gave rise to the name *diabolos* (Greek for 'slanderer' or 'opposing witness'), or Devil; and for the many words for evil spirits in the Old Testament, the Septuagint substituted the Greek *daimonia*, or demons.

Thus a force that had at the outset served as God's instrument for the punishment of sinners (the 'shadow side' of the Old Testament God, Yahweh, as evinced in the Book of Job) evolved from being a *satan* (the Hebrew word *satan* derives from a root meaning 'oppose', 'obstruct', and 'accuse'), into a personality, Satan, whose

OPPOSITE: In this nineteenth-century French copy of a frieze from Persepolis, the Persian religious centre of the Achaemenid Empire, Ahura Mazda, the god of creation, is seen triumphing over the demonic god Angra Mainyu, depicted as a serpent in the panel above, and as a winged beast in the panel below. The Zoroastrian faith is described as Mazdayasna, the worship of Mazda, the embodiment of good, whereas Mainyu is the destroyer of good, the bringer of death and evil personified.

ABOVE: *St Michael* by Raphael (Raffaello Sanzio of Urbino), *c* 1503–5. This Renaissance work was part of a small diptych in the Mazarin collection; the other panel depicted St George fighting the dragon. Here St Michael tramples on the Devil or dragon of Revelation, while evil beasts surround him. In the background a city burns, sinners are cast in leaden coats (left) and figures are bound by serpents (right).

very nature is to oppose, obstruct and accuse. And in the New Testament Satan's role is to obstruct and oppose not just humankind – in which office he is assisted by malevolent spirits, or demons – but also the very kingdom of God, for as long and as effectively as he can.

Naturally, Old Testament and Jewish Apocalyptic ideas about Satan influenced the imagery of the Devil and his minions in the New Testament. The Devil for the New Testament authors was the very embodiment of evil; he was also the wellspring of a band of corrupt spirits, reprising ideas from Apocalyptic literature, which had developed the idea of the Evil One as the head of a host of evil angels. (In the New Testament, the fallen angels, led by Satan, battle the heavenly angels, led by the Archangel Michael, in the Book of Revelation.) The old names, too, are inherited; thus the Evil One is referred to as – most often – Satan or the Devil, but also Belial, Beelzebub, Accuser and Adversary. Satan appears as tempter, deceiver, thwarter and obstructer – perhaps nowhere more clearly so than in the inducements he offers to Jesus to tempt him to abandon his mission to save humankind, as recounted in the synoptic gospels of Matthew, Mark and Luke.

In all the books of the New Testament, however, although his status is greatly increased and references to his power and minions are widespread, no systematic theological framework for Satan is evinced. It was thus left to early theologians and the Church Fathers to flesh out the 'character' of the Devil – to map out a 'biography', as it were, to ascribe a distinct relationship with God and a clear function in day-to-day Christian life. Yet the early church was still grappling with far more fundamental questions, such as the nature of God and the Trinity (Father, Son and Holy Ghost). Its task was further complicated by the plethora of popular apocryphal stories in circulation before the canon of the New Testament was finally established in the 4th century AD; the apocryphal *Books of Adam and Eve* were among several compositions that created a narrative describing and explaining the reasons for Satan's 'fall', in the process fleshing out a psychological persona that would be embellished over the following centuries. Satan's fall as an event was not described in the New Testament.

Perhaps it was because these more pressing debates were continuing that there were no representations either of angels or of Satan and his demons in the first centuries after Christ. The earliest depiction, *c* 520 AD, shows Satan – clad in red – as an angel standing before Christ in a mosaic in San Apollinaire Nuovo in Ravenna, Italy. But as the Western church grew ever more powerful, to become, in RW Southern's opening words to his book *Western Society and the Church in the Middle Ages* (volume two in the Pelican History of the Church series) 'the most elaborate and thoroughly integrated system of religious thought and practice the world has ever known', so the Devil and his cohorts became an increasingly essential part of 'putting a face to evil' – and in the process creating a clear divide between God-fearing Christians, and the pagans and infidels, high among whose ranks the medieval church placed Jews and Saracens, or Muslims.

The decision of the maker of the Ravenna mosaics to clothe Satan in red was a significant one. Red is the colour of blood and fire and, also, of the inhospitable hue of the scorching desert which, for both the ancient Hebrews and Egyptians, could bring failed harvests and famine. Jeffrey Barton Russell notes that 'it is possible that the redness of Seth [the Egyptian god of destruction] helped make red the second most common colour, after black, of the Christian Devil.' It also shows that there was no single image for the artists in the pay of the medieval church to draw on in their depictions of Satan, the Devil and the demonic cohorts. However, medieval tradition held that evil could rarely be disguised behind a benign countenance and, in short, the wicked usually looked wicked. Thus Satan was in medieval imagery often a grotesque combination of man and beast, his outward shape betraying his inner defect. His tell-tale signs are horns, cloven feet, a tail, breath that smells of sulphur, black skin and red eyes; he is lame because of his fall from heaven, and he often also has an extra face on his abdomen, where his genitalia would be, on knees and on buttocks. Artists also looked to the pagan god, Pan, for inspiration, borrowing key attributes – hairy and goat-like, horned and hooved, and often with an oversized phallus; in this manner, many of the old gods of the previous polytheistic religions became the demons of the new faith.

In their images of demons and monstrous beings, however, the same process occurred, with artists

LEFT: A depiction of hell
from the right-hand panel
of the *Triptych of Earthly
Vanity and Divine Salvations*,
by Hans Memling, *c* 1485.
The triptych serves as a
memento mori, presenting
a vision of a female beauty
holding a mirror in the
central panel, flanked by a
skeletal Death on the left
panel and this burning hell
on the right. The devilish
figure has the bestial signs
of cloven hooves, batlike
wings, horns and the
second face on his torso,
a medieval device that
marks him as Satan.

having an even freer hand in their depictions. For, as
well as being represented as the progeny of their ruler,
Satan, and thus stamped with his dreadful likeness,
demons could take almost any shape. And, given the
great surge of artistic interest in Satan, and demons,
that occurred in the twelfth century, a great deal of
creative virtuosity was devoted to depicting demons,
monsters, and Satan himself. Most of all, demons were
hideous – the antithesis (both physically and

spiritually) of the angels – and artists resorted to a
panoply of bestial motifs to make plain their evil, the
monstrous distortions underlining the fact that they
have no true place in the cosmos.

A frequently represented episode in early medieval
art was the fall of Satan and the rebel angels, an event
used not only to explain Satan's origin among the
heavenly cohorts, but also to emphasise the nature of
his sin – for, unlike humankind, who first fell into sin

only when tempted (by the serpent/devil in Paradise), Satan's sin was of the very worst kind, because it was unprovoked. The non-Scriptural explanation being that although one of the highest of the angels, Satan had not been content to worship the Lord, instead desiring the throne of God for himself. Satan's expulsion from heaven was the punishment for his overweening pride. As Satan and his cohorts fall, they are shown becoming blacker as they descend. Hands and feet turn into paws, nails into claws, noses into beaks, beautiful feathered wings become leathery bat wings until their former appearance is unrecognisable as they reach the flames issuing from the jaws of hell, usually portrayed as the monster Leviathan. Here, instead of ethereal paleness (which helps define the angels) they are the colour of black earth; they emanate no light, being essentially a void.

The hideousness of demons is nowhere more apparent than in the Last judgement scenes that were so ubiquitous in the Middle Ages. In carvings, altarpieces and wall paintings, these scenes featured disturbing and frightening images of what would

happen to you if you did not live the life of a good Christian. For the god-fearing medieval mind, the trumpets announcing the start of the final judgement might sound at any moment. Thus it is for good reason that a very large portion of the images in this book are from the medieval period. For, with the beginning of the Renaissance a subtle change starts to take place: increasingly, the emphasis was on analysing the psychological, as well as physical, motivations for human actions. If not yet truly 'scientific', this new approach nevertheless heralded a changing focus – which looked more for rational explanations for man's predicament rather than seeking to explain them by referenced to the actions of 'other', supra-human forces.

BELOW: A seventeenth-century coloured engraving entitled *Hell Broke Loose, or the Murder of Louis* by W. Dent, *c* 1793, presents the guillotine execution of the vilified French king, Louis XVI. A band of menacing dark angels herald his death with drums and trumpets while demonic figures attend the proceedings.

Satan and His Infernal Cohorts

'How art thou fallen from heaven, O Lucifer, son of the morning!'
(Isaiah 14:12)

The use of the word 'Lucifer' in this phrase from the Old Testament book of Isaiah was actually a metaphorical reference to the kingdom of Babylon (or Assyria), likened by the Hebrew prophet to a morning star whose rays are being eclipsed by the rising sun. Yet this 'fallen star' would come to be associated more readily with the figure of the Devil, or Satan – an association reinforced by passages in Ezekiel (28:16) that detail the expulsion of one who was 'profane' from the 'mountain of God'. For early Christians, Jesus' words, 'I saw Satan falling like lightning from heaven', recounted in Luke's gospel (10:18), seemed to confirm the deeper significance of the above verse from Isaiah – that Satan was a fallen angel, ruined by his own iniquity (later, Jesus' words were understood also to predict the final, Christian victory over Satan).

Such biblical references did not offer a clear story of the 'Evil One', however, and it was one task of the early Fathers of the Church to explain more clearly both the origins of Satan, and his role and function in Christian belief. Accordingly, a picture emerged of Lucifer as having been one of the highest angels in heaven – possibly the highest and brightest (Lucifer means 'Light-Bearer'). Becoming puffed up with a sense of his own beauty, Lucifer began to covet the throne of God, and for this overweening, rebellious pride was thrown out of heaven. Early theologians pointed to another passage from Ezekiel in support of this theory: 'Thou hast corrupted thy wisdom by reason of thy brightness' (Ezekiel 14:17). Isaiah was in no doubt as to the punishment for this, writing of Lucifer being 'brought down to hell, to the sides of the pit' (Isaiah 14:15). And, as already noted, Ezekiel reports the Lord as saying, 'I will cast thee as profane out of the mountain of God: and I will destroy thee' (Ezekiel 28:16).

In the emerging 'biography' of the Devil, Satan did not fall alone. Rallying other rebellious angels around him, a battle was waged in heaven between the angels (headed by the archangel Michael) and the rebel angels, during which Satan and his cohorts were expelled from paradise – ignominiously 'falling' towards hell. (In *Paradise Lost*, Milton makes the rebellion and expulsion from heaven last nine days.) Artistic depictions of the episode show the rebel angels becoming blacker and more hideous as they fall, acquiring tails, horns and talons in their descent. Finally, in hell, the fallen angels are entirely demonic, coal-black and hideous – with Satan the most hideous-looking of them all.

Unable to regain heaven, Satan and his foot soldiers wreak vengeance on God's creation, humankind, corrupting through false promises and deceptive appearances. Thus in the Garden of Eden Satan takes the forms of a serpent, 'more subtil than any beast of the field' (Genesis 3:1). For the medieval Christian, the demons who served as Satan's henchmen were very real, and to be feared; and the medieval artists' portrayals of them – as tempters on earth, and tormentors in hell – would be unequalled in their grisliness.

ABOVE: This version of the popular story of the torments Saint Anthony suffered in the desert at the hands of demons is from a fifteenth-century French illuminated manuscript of the *Golden Legend* by Jacobus de Voragine – a work that was a rich retelling of biblical stories and lives of the saints, and whose contents furnished medieval and later artists with much pictorial material. Here, the demons include a basilisk-cum-dragon and a hissing, insect-like demon with crab-like claws. The placing of a second face on the blue demon's abdomen was a common medieval means of designating Satan and his fiendish cohorts; here, a dangling tongue is in lieu of the male member, while the black demon's bizarre, curling appendage hints at the erotic nature of some of the saint's hallucinations. The reader of this work would have been in no doubt as to the outcome of this demonic assault, however – in the gold letter 'A' below this image (not seen), Anthony is shown being blessed by a fellow saint.

OPPOSITE: In *The Temptation of Saint Anthony*, 1512–16, by Matthias Grünewald, the ascetic saint is tormented by a ghastly horde of demons with monstrous features in this panel from the elaborate Isenheim Altarpiece, which provides a pictorial commentary on the manifestation of evil in the world and its eventual defeat through the Resurrection, with its promise of eternal life. A bird with arms wields a club, a basilisk (a fabled creature that was half snake and half cock) with a cock's body, but four legs instead of a snake's coil, bites the hermit's hand, while a demon with horns and bat's wings tugs at his white hair. A blotchy, imp-like demon with a bloated stomach sits on the book of sacred scriptures with which the saint fortifies his resolve. Other murky demons loom in the dark space directly above the saint's head – horrible portents of the torments that may yet lie in store for Saint Anthony.

OPPOSITE: Adam and Eve stand either side of the Tree of the Knowledge of Good and Evil, among whose branches slithers the tempter serpent, Satan, here given a beguiling female face, *c* 1520. Eve has already taken the first bite of the apple, and hands it to her companion, whose dark expression betrays his inner turmoil, torn as he is between obeying God and his overwhelming desire for Eve, by whom he is mesmerized. It is clear that they have encountered their first awakening of sexual desire; now, aware of their nakedness, both clutch fig leaves to cover their private parts. The stem of this apple resembles an iron spike more than a stalk, and the female snake gazes at it with an awful intensity, as though contemplating all the miseries that will now befall humankind.

ABOVE: The unknown fourteenth-century German illustrator who produced this miniature made no bones about the identity of the corrupting snake in the Garden of Eden – for this is Satan himself, with his crown and bat-like wings; his lower half alone has the shape of a serpent. Knowing that the only thing forbidden to Adam and Eve in the Garden of Eden was the fruit of the Tree of the Knowledge of Good and Evil, the serpent lured Eve with the promise of knowledge ('your eyes will be opened and you will be like gods knowing both good and evil'). Eve ate the fruit then gave it to Adam to share, their sinful disobedience precipitating their expulsion from Paradise.

ABOVE: *The Heavy Stone*, one of a series of frescos by Spinello Aretino illustrating scenes from the life of Saint Benedict (*c* 480–550), founder of the Benedictine order. The frescos were painted in 1387–8, and – now restored – may still be viewed in the sacristy of the basilica of San Miniato al Monte, perched on a hill above Florence.

Borrowed from the *Golden Legend* by Jacobus de Voragine, this episode illustrates the popular tale of how the monks, when building their church, tried to lift a stone but found it too heavy to budge. Upon which, Saint Benedict made a sign of the Cross, and the stone was raised with ease – revealing the Devil skulking beneath it.

LEFT: A page from an fourteenth-century illuminated manuscript of Dante's *Divine Comedy*, which was written between 1308 and 1321, the year of the Florentine poet's death. Divided into three *canticas*, or parts (Hell, Purgatory, Paradise), the first-person narrative recounts the story, in verse, of Dante's journey through the three realms of the dead during Holy Week, 1300. He is accompanied through hell and Purgatory by the Latin poet Virgil. Here, Virgil shows Dante the Inferno, hell itself, in which the terrifying figure of Satan is devouring the naked souls of the damned. Dante's detailed conception of the underworld strongly influenced the medieval world's view of the afterlife, and fuelled the imagination of artists for centuries to come – continuing long after the notion of eternal damnation had loosened its grip on the popular imagination.

RIGHT: In this engraving by Gustave Doré, Dante and Virgil are beset by demons swarming up from the deep chasms in the eighth circle of hell on their passage through the Inferno – the first part of Dante's *Divine Comedy*. Dante's Inferno comprised nine circles, detailed in ascending order of awfulness; the eighth (*cantos* 18–30) – the *malebolge* – is thus very deep, nearing the centre of the earth and Satan himself. The *malebolge* was in turn subdivided into ten descending concentric circles, where those guilty of fraudulence (such as the seducers, flatterers and panderers) were punished. Here Virgil (recognizable by his crown of laurels) wards off Malacoda, leader of the fiends, between chasms five and six where, respectively, the corrupt politicians and the hypocrites are tormented.

ABOVE: Sir Joseph Noel Paton, *Satan Watching the Sleep of Christ*, 1874. Satan here is a massive, brooding, all-too real presence, with flames issuing from his tousled head, their red tongues forming an infernal crown. He is pensive, furious – quite literally fuming – and evidently stumped as to how to penetrate Christ's almost perceptible shroud of holiness. Although he is huge and pictorially dominant, it is the supine, delicate figure of Christ that emanates real power, even asleep. The episode of Christ's time in the wilderness, and the clash at its conclusion between supreme good and supreme evil, is rendered in graspable human terms. Sir Noel Paton was a Scottish painter who was heavily influenced by the artists of the Pre-Raphaelite school, and this picture is in the style of the religious paintings on which he concentrated after 1870.

OPPOSITE: A detail from *The Preaching and Deeds of the Antichrist* (1499–1502/3) by Luca Signorelli, a fresco in the San Brizio Chapel in the Cathedral in Orvieto, Italy. This central portion of the fresco shows the Antichrist, directed by the Devil himself, as the false preacher. The Antichrist's garb and pose resemble traditional images of Christ preaching to his followers, apart from for the two protruding tufts of hair that suggest devilish horns. His body is also clasped tightly by the Devil, who feeds the Antichrist his lines; indeed, the two figures are so closely intertwined that the Antichrist's left arm and pointing finger perfectly follow the line of the Devil's same limb – revealing that they are one and the same. Beneath the Antichrist's pedestal are piled the gold and precious artefacts with which he plans to seduce his onlookers.

ABOVE: These three demons who stand looking aghast can be found in one of the fourteenth-century frescos by Andrea di Buonaiuto (known as Andrea da Firenze) in the Chapel of the Spaniards in the church of Santa Maria Novella in Florence, Italy. Through wrung hands and an anxious, furrowed brow (red demon), palms clapped on the face in horrified astonishment (yellow demon) and fingers poised on a mouth which is gaping in shock (blue demon), they express their astonishment at Christ's descent into the netherworld of Limbo. Christ has come to free the souls of the righteous who died before his time on earth, and who were therefore deprived of the possibility of Christian salvation. The demons are terrified at the prospect of their infernal domain, the flames of which surround them, licking the rocks on either side them which have been rent asunder.

RIGHT: A devil from the so-called 'Grand Etteilla' – a set of Tarot cards originally published in 1789. Etteilla was the name adopted by Jean-Baptiste Alliette (Etteilla is Alliette spelt backwards), a French occultist who was instrumental in the early development of the esoteric Tarot, by which the cards were used for divination purposes. Etteilla was the first to publish a deck purely for occult purposes. This card – number 14 in the Etteilla pack; 15 in the Tarot deck – represents *Force Majeure* (Absolute Necessity), or the Devil. The Devil is depicted as part Pan, the half-goat god of nature, and part scaly, winged demon. In the Tarot the Devil symbolizes temptation and excess, particularly in terms of earthly desires – in other words, the unconscious, or 'shadow' self.

ABOVE: *The Devil presenting Saint Augustine with the Book of Vices* (c 1480) by the Austrian Northern Renaissance painter Michael Pacher. This panel from the Altarpiece of the Church Fathers shows Saint Augustine – one of the four Latin (Western) Fathers – in his full bishop's regalia, including mitre and crosier. In the altarpiece he appears with the other Latin Fathers (Ambrose, Gregory and Jerome). According to the *Golden Legend*, the book that the Devil presents to Augustine was a written documentation of all the vices and failures in the history of mankind – one of which was the saint's failure to recite a particular prayer. The Devil is portrayed with goatish hooves, deer's antlers, bony vertebrae and reptilian wings, and with a second face on his posterior. Through the power of prayer, however, the saint has caused his page to be erased from the book of vices and confronts the Devil with a look of serenity and resolve. The Devil is visibly enraged, and begins to spout fire from his ring-shaped ears.

ABOVE: This detail of the damned being forced into hell by dark-skinned demons is from a painted panel of the Last Judgement (c 1431–5) by Fra Angelico in the Museo di San Marco in Florence, Italy. Fra Angelico produced several altarpieces on the theme of Christ's final judgement, but in no other are the demons so numerous or fiendishly hell-bent. With blazing eyes, jagged teeth and furious expressions, they torment and torture the sinners, whose ranks include bishops, courtiers, kings and cardinals. Using pitchforks and hooks, they shove and tug at them, pitching them into a multi-chambered hell presided over by Satan himself (see page 166). One demon even prepares to sink his fangs into the neck of a woman whom he holds fast by the hair.

RIGHT: Illustration from the *Livre de la Vigne de Nostre Seigneur, c* 1450–70, Bodleian Library, Oxford, an illustrated work on the Antichrist, the Last Judgement, Heaven and Hell. This illustration shows a demon punishing the naked souls of the proud and vainglorious by torturing them on a wheel in hell. The infernal creature has long horns, talons, a tail, a snout, long ears, and a particularly nasty leer – positively relishing the torments of the damned. He sports several extra faces; two on his abdomen, and more on his elbows and knees. Jeffrey Burton Russell notes in his *Lucifer* that horns were the most common animal feature of the Devil in medieval times, being an ancient symbol of power; the second being the tail and the third being wings.

OPPOSITE (BELOW): Demons were frequently involved in the seduction or impregnation of women. In this illustration from a medieval manuscript, a horned demon with a goatish visage is shown assaulting a sleeping woman, while other bestial-looking demons prance above his head. In medieval bestiaries, the goat was described as a lascivious animal, and the attribution of a goat's beard is thus particularly appropriate here; the beards commonly worn by gods in classical art have similar sexual connotations. The demons in the upper register have extra orifices in the form of small faces positioned at their knee joints, and their tongues are shown hanging out – such agitated 'openness' also suggesting lasciviousness.

ABOVE: Detail of a stained glass window dating from 1884 to be found in the church at Sognolles-en-Montois, Seine et Marne, France. Depicting the weighing of the souls at the Last Judgement, the pane shows the Devil, in the form of a dragon, trying to upset the scales of justice in which the souls of the dead are being weighed by Saint Michael, the most active adversary of the Devil. A tongue of fire issues from his beaked mouth. The Devil is actually holding onto the golden chain, preparing to give it a good tug, with his other reptilian hand grasping the pan in which the tiny souls are praying. But, given the calm demeanour of these naked souls, it seems they are destined to be saved, and thus the Devil cannot possess himself of the number of victims he had counted upon.

OMNIPOTENS

OPPOSITE: This illustration of Anthony the Great, saint, hermit and founder of monasticism, being tormented by demons is from the *Sforza Hours*, an illuminated manuscript made in Italy in the late fifteenth century. Painted by Giovan Pietro Birago, this page reveals some fantastically colourful and fiendish demons for the contemplation of the wealthy reader of this jewel-like book of hours. Tormenting the saint with clubs and forks, the demons take the form of ghastly composite creatures – with twisted horns, unnatural breasts, snouts, webbed feet and tendrils reminiscent of some sea creature; one demon (bottom left) is a coiled snake below the waist. Ghastliest of all, though, is the two-toned demon on the upper-left, with his bat wings, upturned fangs, a sprouting second pair of horns, and a second face on his abdomen. The *Sforza Hours* can be seen at the British Library, London.

ABOVE: A coloured engraving by the German Renaissance artist Martin Schöngauer (c 1445–91) depicting *Saint Anthony Tormented by Demons*, c 1470–5. In this ghastly, airborne evocation of the popular devotional subject of the torments suffered by Anthony, the hermit saint displays a stoical indifference to the onslaught by these grotesque creatures to be found in no place on God's earth. The frenzied demons batter him with sticks and snatch at his limbs, hair and clothes, yet the saint's brow is untroubled, his gaze serene. This was one of Schöngauer's earliest prints, and it was extremely influential; Giorgio Vasari wrote that Michelangelo made a colour drawing of the work when he was just 13.

ABOVE: The *Temptation of Saint Anthony* (c 1875–7) by the French post-Impressionist painter Paul Cézanne, Musée d'Orsay, Paris, France. The temptations suffered here are clearly erotic, yet demonic in origin – the 'master of ceremonies' is a horned, comic-opera devil. Anthony holds up his arms to shield his gaze from the naked woman who unveils her flesh to distract him from prayer and who, with a luminous brilliance, occupies the centre of the composition. The landscape resembles Provence rather than a desert waste and Cézanne has, unusually for this subject, included small putti reminiscent of cherubs. Theodore Reff has noted that the work was painted shortly after the publication of Flaubert's novella, *Temptation of Saint Anthony* (*La Tentation de Saint Antoine*; 1874), in which a cortege accompanies the brazen seductress.

OPPOSITE: An illustration showing the various actions of devils from the *Breviari d'Amor*, a French illuminated manuscript written by Matfré Ermengau of Béziers in the second half of the fourteenth century. In the top register is depicted the fall of the rebellious angels into the Leviathan's (hell's) mouth, with God enthroned. In the middle register, an enthroned devil dispatches two other devils to their work: one, a temptation to lust, stands behind an embracing couple; the other, a temptation to avarice, pours money into the robe of a crowned woman. In the bottom register is depicted the temptation to robbery (shown as a soldier stripping the cloak off a youth and threatening him with a dagger), the temptation to wrath (depicted as two men quarrelling) and devils on the stern and mast of a ship, causing a tempest.

Elloza dla art dl diable co tebre les gens. Lo pricep dls diables en uia sos min

Tempta p̄ luxuria. | tempta per auaricia. | Tempta p̄ roberia. | Tempta p̄ ira. | Oroue tēpesta p̄ negat

Satan and His Infernal Cohorts

Satan and His Infernal Cohorts

LEFT: This painting by Henry Fuseli, entitled *Nightmare*, caused a sensation when it was exhibited in 1782, and was much reproduced in prints of the time. The notion that sleep was a fragile state in which the unconscious sleeper – especially the female sleeper – could fall prey to an attack by evil spirits was a well-established one. Male demons, known as incubi, had sexual relations with sleeping women to draw off their energy. Although the incubus had a female counterpart in the shape of the succubus, more often than not it was the female victim, tortured by nocturnal visions, who was the subject – with all its titillating possibilities – of choice for male artists.

CBelial ſtans ante infernum habens
cõſilium cum cõmunitate dÿabolica ⋆

ABOVE: A woodcut illustration from *Das Buch Belial* (1473) by Jacobus de Teramo. The woodcut shows the demon Belial consulting with fellow demons at the gates of hell, represented as the mouth of Leviathan. Other woodcuts in the book make it plain that Belial was one of the demons in the Solomonic tradition, and Solomon looms large in the narrative. According to this ancient piece of lore, Belial was one of the four chief demons (along with Bileth, Asmodeus and Gaap) to be imprisoned in a brass vessel by the magic ring of King Solomon. In *Paradise Lost*, Belial is one of the principal devils in hell, possessed of great learning and faculty for argument.

OPPOSITE: Beelzebub and other demons, from the *Livre de la Vigne Nostre Seigneur*, *c* 1450–70. This was the image of the Prince of Hell common throughout the Middle Ages – a demon of foul physical appearance; a hideous hodge-podge of a beast fashioned from features of different creatures. Beelzebub and his demonic cohorts sport horns, tails, furry pelts, wings and scales, and extra faces (here, on the abdomen, knees and shoulders, from which sprout scaly arms and bird-like lower limbs and talons). All wield flesh hooks with which to grapple and torture the damned in hell; all are naked (a sign of barbarity); and all are tinged with unnatural colouring. Lucifer's head sprouts further demonic protuberances, forming a nest-like helmet of horned carbuncles. The collector Francis Douce, into whose hands the medieval manuscript eventually came, is reported to have exclaimed that such head attire 'should seem to be a tower of Babel!'

OPPOSITE: William Blake, *Satan Arousing the Rebel Angels*, 1808. This watercolour was one of a series of illustrations that Blake produced for an early nineteenth-century edition of Milton's *Paradise Lost* (1667). Satan is depicted as an athletic young man among other unclothed and equally muscular youths – a recognisable human being in the mould of a classical hero from Antiquity. In this, Blake was much influenced by the art of Michelangelo, and in particular the Sistine Chapel frescos. Eluding all labels, Blake's art – like his poetry – was visionary, reflecting his highly personal aesthetics. His pictorial works were stimulated by literary sources, including Dante, Milton and the Bible, as well as by his own poetry.

ABOVE: William Blake, *The Good and Evil Angels, c* 1795–1805. Blake was a profoundly religious man, albeit of a nonconformist bent, and believed that the artist's role was to reveal the realm of the spirit, which he saw as concealed behind the tangible world of the senses. He possessed a mystical belief in truth as something revealed, not learned. In this image, he depicted two heroically proportioned figures struggling over a child, whom the figure on the right (the Good Angel) has snatched from the clutches of the sightless, suspended figure of the Evil angel. Dark-skinned with his foot in chains and surrounded by flames, the latter is the Prince of hell or one of his cohorts. The precise meaning of the picture, with its abstract landscape of sea and setting (or possibly rising) sun, is still a subject of controversy.

ABOVE: Known as the *Estatua del Angel Caido* (Statue of the Fallen Angel), this sculptural representation of Lucifer – the only public monument to Satan in Spain and, it is said, in the world – was erected in the Retiro Park in Madrid, Spain, in 1874. It was made by the sculptor Ricardo Bellver. Lucifer is shown as a Herculean youth, howling with rage and loss at having been cast from heaven; he is bound by the coils of a snake, emblem of his own evil.

LEFT: This 'portrait' of Satan is from a painting by the Swiss-born artist Johann Heinrich Füssli (1741–1825), who became known, following his acceptance into the Royal Academy of Art in London in 1790, as Henry Fuseli. The painting (c 1790–1800) is entitled *Satan Reflects on his Deeds* and illustrates verses from Book IV of Milton's *Paradise Lost*. Dark and brooding, this figure of Satan is a psychologically powerful portrayal of loss and the banishment of hope – conjuring Milton's lines, 'And like a Devilish engine back recoils/Upon himself; horror and doubt distract/ His troubled thoughts, and from the bottom stir/The Hell within him; for within him Hell/He brings.' Fuseli was arguably the first artist to promote the image of Satan as a heroically proportioned figure, a depiction that influenced the iconography of the Romantics.

LEFT: A colour plate with a 'portrait' of Satan, from a book by the Swiss writer and protestant pastor Johann Caspar Lavater (1741–1801) entitled *Essai sur la physiognomie (Essay on Physiognomy)*, 1776. Although a belief in the correlation between physical features and character traits was widely held at the time, Lavater reinvigorated the 'folk science' of physiognomy; he studied real portraits rather than ascribing animal features to faces as the 'caricatures' of his predecessors had done. Believing that the face was the mirror of the soul, the turbulence of Satan's 'black soul' is clearly visible on this 'portrait', with its sickly, greenish tinge of envy coupled with pride.

LEFT: A detail of the *Last Judgement* altarpiece (*c* 1431) by Fra Angelico, shown on page 153. Fra Angelico conjured a terrifying vision of Satan in the pit of hell in this tempera on panel, furiously chewing on the naked sinners whose blood pours out of his three demonic mouths and nostrils. Satan is presented as a darkly monstrous lumpen creature, with lifeless, bestial eyes; the liquid of the cauldron in which he sits, stewing, is constantly stirred by demons.

ABOVE: *The Last Judgement*, *c* 1480, a detail from a panel painting called the Wenhaston Doom, from St Peter's Church in Wenhaston, England. A doom painting shows the final judgement of souls after death and here the Archangel Michael weighs the souls while Satan argues the weight of sins. Hidden for hundreds of years under layers of whitewash applied during the Reformation, the panel, which was above the chancel arch, was discovered in 1889 when rain washed away the paint to reveal the unusually well-preserved and vividly coloured images. The entire piece depicts several judgement scenes, split by blank areas, one of which can be seen to the left of the image here, where a great crucifix would have been fixed.

RIGHT: Sir Thomas Lawrence, *Satan and Beelzebub*, 1795–7. The drawing, in black chalk with white highlights on brown paper, was a preparatory study for the painter's reception piece at the Royal Academy in London in 1797. Lawrence depicts the two as monumental figures and in the antique manner (both are naked, and Satan sports a winged helmet); they fill the composition with their dark, towering presence. Satan (left) erupts, his arms raised in a gesture of power; Beelzebub plants both hands on a spear. This was the image of Satan that so appealed to the Romantic imagination – the proud rebel, a figure of darkness, but also of melodramatic grandeur. For these were ingredients of 'the sublime', with its – to the Romantics – delightful, frisson-provoking mix of repulsion and pleasure, and sense of 'noble ruin'.

RIGHT: An illustration (*c* 1799) of Satan and Beelzebub in hell in the Lake with Liquid Fire. The lake of fire fuelled by brimstone (sulfur) is referred to in Revelation as the place of final judgement for Satan and the damned ('And the devil that deceived them was cast into the lake of fire and brimstone, where the beast and the false prophet are,' Revelation 20:10). In Book 1 of John Milton's *Paradise Lost*, Satan and his second-in-command, Beelzebub, lie prostrate in this fiery lake, which gives off darkness instead of light, and into which they and the other rebel angels have been cast after being defeated by God in heaven.

OPPOSITE: An engraving by Gustave Doré; one of a series illustrating a nineteenth-century edition of Milton's *Paradise Lost*. This plate shows Satan and Beelzebub just after their fall from heaven; they have been cast by God into a lake of liquid fire in the 'bottomless pit'. But even in defeat Satan's unrepentant evil nature is searching for a target; after consultation with his infernal cohorts, he will decide to seek revenge on God by corrupting His new beloved race – the human beings, Adam and Eve. Contrary to tradition, Doré's fallen angels retain some of their handsomeness; for traditional iconography – and Milton's verses – had it that Lucifer's beauty was totally and irredeemably destroyed as a result of the fall.

ABOVE: An illustration of the demon Belphegor, from Colin de Plancy's *Dictionnaire Infernal*, 1925. A demon of ingenious inventions and discoveries, the influence of Belphegor was also sometimes ascribed to misogynists and licentious men. The name was a corruption of the biblical name Baal-Peor, the god of the Moabites, neighbours of the Israelites when they were camped on the plains of Moab. The Old Testament book of Numbers (chapter 25) tells of how the Israelites had illicit relations with the Moabite women and sacrificed to their god. As a punishment Moses ordered all those who had sacrificed to Baal-Peor to be killed (24,000 in all; Numbers 25:9). The Moab god thus became a Hebrew symbol of abomination; indeed, throughout history, deities of hostile nations have been transformed into symbols of fiendish superstition.

OPPOSITE: One of a series of five drawings by Peter Paul Rubens relating to his painting the *Fall of the Damned*, 1620. In this preparatory drawing for the central portion of his large canvas, Rubens shows the men and women who are damned to an eternity in hell at the final judgement as a vortex of tumbling, biting, clawing flesh. The demons are so intertwined with the bodies of the fallen that they are almost indistinguishable from them, yet a second glance reveals the giveaway pointed ears, horns, tails and wings. One demon, which bears the enormous, startled-looking naked woman, binds her with snake-like coils where his legs would be. Above, unfortunate souls cover their heads in shame. The dramatic chiaroscuro (contrast of light and dark) effects heighten the sense of a downward spiral into the abyss.

The Path of Evil

In the previous chapter we saw how demons, Satan's henchmen, were depicted as the antithesis in every way of the angels, the heavenly host, and how from early medieval times Western artists employed a rich panoply of motifs to underscore the demonic and bestial – and, crucially, pagan – nature of the infernal cohorts in the Devil's pay.

Just as the saints were very real as intermediaries between mortals and their Creator for medieval Christians, so Satan and his cohorts were ubiquitous as Satan's representatives on earth – as tormentors and afflicters of the 'children of man'. In the mind of the medieval Christian demons were everywhere, and to be feared all the more for the masks they wore. In his sixth-century *Dialogues*, Saint Gregory the Great (then Pope Gregory) had written at length of over-active demons, warning against their influence. In his work *Moralia in Job* (Commentary on Job) Gregory had also compiled a list of Seven Deadly Sins which, in increasing order of seriousness, consisted of: *luxuria* (over-extravagance, later becoming lust); *gula* (gluttony); *tristia* (sadness); *avaritia* (avarice); *ira* (anger); *invidia* (envy); and *superbia* (pride, or hubris). These were drawn from earlier (fourth- and fifth-century) compilations of offences and harmful passions elaborated by the Greek monastic theologian Evagrius of Pontus (*b* 345), in his Eight Evil Thoughts, and Saint John Cassian, writing of the Eight Principal Vices, *c* 420–9. The fifth-century *Psychomachia* or Battle for the Soul by Prudentius was also influential in the establishment of a 'canon' of virtues and vices. For Gregory, as for the earlier writers, the sins' escalating severity represented an increasing absorption with the self (and the offences against love that this engenders), with pride the most egregious of all sins. Sadness was later replaced by *acedia* (spiritual sloth) – putting off what God asks of his human creation.

In the Middle Ages, the Seven Deadly Sins were important in demonstrating to the lay community how the Devil operated through temptation, the more effectively to encourage resistance to it. Thus each deadly sin had its contrary virtue – chastity being the opposite of lust, moderation the opposite of gluttony, generosity the opposite of avarice (greed) and so forth, with Christian humility the opposite of pride (it was pride, after all, that sparked the fall of Lucifer from heaven, and self-love distracted from the Christian devotion properly due to God). Numerous saints' lives – in particular that of Saint Anthony, the hermit saint who famously suffered a battery of demonic assaults in the desert – also existed to illustrate and explain the ways and wiles of the Devil in his attempts to claim human souls.

Of course, the earliest temptation of humankind dated to Genesis. In persuading Eve to eat the apple from the 'tree of the knowledge of good and evil' in the Garden of Eden, the Devil in the shape of a serpent precipitated the expulsion of Adam and Eve from the garden – and, due to 'The Fall', Adam and Eve, and all of humankind after them, were consigned to strive and suffer, and die. Humanity's moral failure meant that mortals were sorely in need of redemption.

ABOVE: In this stained-glass window in Lincoln Cathedral, Lincoln, England, Eve is shown taking the apple from the serpent and handing it to Adam to share. The fruit of the Tree of Knowledge of Good and Evil was the only thing forbidden to Adam and Eve by God, their Creator, in the Garden of Eden. Yet Satan, in the guise of a serpent, on learning of this, spies that this is a way to bring about the fall of humankind and so avenge himself on God. The tempter snake entices Eve with the prospect of knowledge, all the while flattering her vanity. Eating the forbidden fruit will bring pain and death into the world: Eve, and all women after her, will suffer the pain of childbirth; Adam, and all men after him, must toil for food. Both will feel heat and cold – paradise has been lost.

ABOVE: William Blake, *Eve Tempted by the Serpent*, 1799–1800. This fantastically imagined Garden of Eden, painted in the experimental style of gum and gold on copper (and thus, regrettably, now deteriorating), is a depiction that could only have sprung from the rich and uniquely personal furrows of Blake's extraordinary imagination, although the story is drawn from the book of Genesis in the Old Testament. In Blake's representation the serpent has taken on gargantuan proportions and yet Eve appears unconcerned by it, even though its monstrous coils circle her feet like a noose. She is intent only on reaching up for the forbidden fruit with which the snake is tempting her. By provoking this single act of disobedience, Satan will succeed in his plan to corrupt humankind, God's perfect creation. Nearby, his head also circled by the serpent's coils, the sleeping Adam is unaware of impending doom.

The Path of Evil 51

OPPOSITE: Francisco de Goya, *Witches' Sabbath*, 1797–8. A huge ram – the archetypal image of the Devil – sits among a group of witches, demanding one of the children as a sacrifice. The garland of vine leaves around his horns recalls the old heathen cult of Pan, with all its ancient, orgiastic rituals in honour of the pagan god. An emaciated child is offered to the he-goat, though the infant has barely more flesh on him than the skeletal form of the child lying on the ground on the left. From a witch's skewer are strung the bodies of dead infants. A swarm of bats overshadows the day and darkens the sky at this Sabbat, or great gathering of witches. By this picture Goya was in fact mocking the superstitious beliefs of credulous old women such as these hags. The painting can be seen in the Museo Lazaro Galdiano in Madrid, Spain.

ABOVE: An eighteenth-century print of a nocturnal Sabbat, or witches' great gathering, with the dancing line of novice witches led by a fire-demon with horns and the goatish lower body of a satyr. Smoke, cauldrons and fire abound, and demons, demonic creatures and he-goats are multiplied throughout the chaotic scene. In the centre is a seated ram, raised on a pedestal, its posterior being kissed by a witch-candidate in an *Osculum infame*, or Kiss of Shame. A witch flies on a pitchfork, having gained the power of transvection through the pact formed with the Devil. The Sabbat harked back to pagan Dionysiac rituals, which would culminate in an orgiastic feast that would last until the cock crowed.

The Path of Evil | 53

ABOVE: A Roman satyr depicted in mosaic, from the Villa Romana del Casale in the Piazza Armerina, Sicily. The satyr was a mythological creature who was half-man and half-goat. This example, dating from the third century AD, has many of the traits that later artists would adopt in their renderings of the Devil – goatish horns, large pointed ears, hairy legs and cloven hooves. As companions of Bacchus, the Roman god of wine, satyrs were associated with inebriation and physical pleasure. Given the early Church's strictures against fornication and excess, it was not surprising that satyrs were demonized and associated – along with other pagan spirits – with the Devil.

OPPOSITE: This illustration from *The Astrologer of the Nineteenth Century* (1825) highlights the upsurge of interest in occultism in the nineteenth century. For although ostensibly about astrology, the volume was in truth more concerned with the power of the astrologer to conjure up spirits from the other world. The astrologer-sorcerer seems safe within the magic circle he has created, beyond which lurk demons, snakes, shadowy birds and insects. The sorcerer kneels before an altar of magical charts, and seems to be enjoying the protection of an angel. The demons appear to marvel, and also to be thwarted – but for how long they will remain so is not clear.

OPPOSITE: This late medieval woodcut dates from *c* 1489, and appeared in a book by Ulrich Molitor entitled *De Lamiis et Pythonicis et Mulieribus.* It shows the Devil making advances to seduce a witch, whose diabolical practices – so it was claimed by witch-hunters – included deviant sexuality and coupling with the Devil. Women were seen as far more susceptible to the Devil's advances than men, and the Church's belief that Satan worship existed, and was widespread, gave rise to infamous witch trials during which 'confessions' were extracted – usually under torture. It was around the time of this woodcut, in around 1500, that full-scale persecution and burnings began.

ABOVE: In this woodcut, made after an original by the German artist Albrecht Dürer, a demon is shown dragging a child off into the Devil's service, having paid his parents for the privilege. The Devil, it was popularly believed, had a fondness for young flesh, and the notion that children were sacrificed in satanic rituals fuelled the hysteria in late medieval times that witches were 'midwives' who 'delivered' children over to the Devil to be human sacrifices at the Sabbat, or great gathering of witches.

OPPOSITE (ABOVE): Woodcut miniature from the *Chroniques de Saint-Denis* (*Chronicles of Saint Denis*), a thirteenth-century manuscript from the medieval monastery of the same name in northern France. The royal abbey of Saint-Denis, whose most famous ecclesiastic was Abbot Suger (d. 1151), was a fabulously wealthy and powerful institution in the Middle Ages; the abbey become the burial place for the kings of France. It was a renowned centre of learning; its Benedictine monks collected and copied manuscripts and also made their own contributions to monastic literature – monks, after all, as 'soldiers of Christ' had a duty to lead their people to salvation. In this illustration, a brother is shown saving a magician from the clutches of the Devil, with whom the foolish man had made a pact.

OPPOSITE (BELOW): An engraving after the frontispiece of Christopher Marlowe's *The Tragicall Historie of the Life and Death of Doctor Faustus*, 1616. The historical figure of Johann Faust, born in Germany *c* 1480, is the most infamous person in modern times to have – allegedly – sold his soul to the Devil. He is said to have been a teacher, physician, barber and magician but, above all, a scientist with a boundless thirst for knowledge. According to the legend that grew up after his death in approximately 1540, it was in exchange for the highest knowledge, including the secret of life itself, that Faust sold his soul to the Devil. All this marvellous knowledge would come to nothing, however, since the Devil had reserved a terrible end for Faust.

ABOVE: Hieronymus Bosch (*c* 1450–1516), *Temptation of Saint Anthony*. Bosch returned to the themes of temptation, doubt and the ever-waiting trap repeatedly in his art, and in particular in his portrayals of the hallucinatory tribulations suffered by the hermit-saint Anthony the Great. Here, as in his other Saint Anthony panels, the inclusion of demonic insects and fantastical animals serves to underline Bosch's belief – in common with other late medieval minds – that temptation was a physical as well as a spiritual assault by demons. The realism with which the demonic creatures are depicted accentuates the saint's suffering, and Anthony's eventual triumph over them will thus be a hard-won victory, earned through prayer and stoicism.

OPPOSITE AND RIGHT: The Hay Wain and Hell, the central and right panels of the triptych *The Hay Wain*, *c* 1485–90, by Hieronymus Bosch. The gigantic hay wain (cart) – the hay representing mammon – is here a symbol of towering human greed and of a human race given over to sin, completely neglectful of God's law and unaware of the fate that awaits it. The hay wain rolls across the landscape, pulled by demons towards their hellish cousins in the Inferno (see right, one of Bosch's earliest depictions of Hell). Yet the humans who worship the hay appear utterly unaware that their sinful folly will lead them to torment in the afterlife. On top of the haystack, to the right of the music-making and amorous couples, a demon plays his nose as a trumpet. For all the brawling and clamour beneath them, it would appear that the lovers are the greatest fools, believing themselves to be safe on top of the rolling haystack.

ABOVE: Francisco de Goya, *Asmodea* (also called *Asmodeus – Fantastic Vision*), 1820–3. This unsettling picture is one of the 'Black Paintings' that Goya painted directly on to the walls of his home, the Quinta del Sordo. The group of 14 works were so dubbed because of their dark tones and the nightmarish visions they expressed. All are disturbing depictions of a saturnine artistic temperament. In this scene of menacing, flying figures, Asmodea – a demon associated with lasciviousness – has claimed an unwilling victim for his demonic flight, during which he lifts the roofs of the houses over which they fly to reveal the previously concealed lustful activities of their inhabitants. His companion is clearly terrified, his open mouth conveying all the horror of the nightmare, with its speed of flight – indicated by the billowing fabric and windswept hair – and vertiginous height.

ABOVE: Hieronymus Bosch ((c 1450–1516), *The Seven Deadly Sins,* 1475–80, a painted tabletop now in the Prado museum in Madrid, Spain. The segments of the central roundel – which are arranged around an iris with Christ as the all-seeing pupil at the centre of the 'eye' – illustrate the Seven Deadly Sins, and their effects on the human community. In the four smaller medallions in the corners of the tabletop are illustrations of the Four Last Things (Death, Judgement, Heaven, Hell). Christ directs the viewer's gaze towards Sloth (represented by a man sleeping in his chair); next, reading clockwise, is Lust, under cover of a tent; Pride (or Vanity) follows; then Anger (giving rise to rape and murder); Envy (shown as a heavy burden) is followed by Greed (a corrupt judge) and Gluttony. Beneath Christ is the ominous inscription *Cave, cave, dominus videt* (Beware, the Lord is watching).

OPPOSITE: This startling scene of violation and decapitation is from a painting by the Flemish artist Herri met de Bles (born c 1510), known as the *The Inferno.* Now in the Palazzo Ducale (Doge's Palace) in Venice, the painting is a fantastical vision of hell, teeming with crackling insects with shiny carapaces and slithering snakes and reptiles, and monstrously deformed phantasmagorical creatures. The hundreds of tiny humans – male and female – are subject to all manner of tortures and degradations; in this detail, in keeping with the notion of *contrapasso* – the punishment fitting the crime – the sinner is perhaps being punished for the sin 'against nature' (and therefore God) of sodomy. Accusations of sodomy often went hand in hand with accusations of heresy, and the sinner may therefore be being punished for this broader – and far graver – offence.

RIGHT: One of a series of 29 engravings, based on drawings by Moritz Retzch, made to illustrate an 1836 German edition of Goethe's play, *Faust*. This plate – the fourth in the book – illustrates the moment where Faust agrees to make a pact with the Devil, who here appears in the shape of Mephistopheles. Faust exclaims that his word should be a sufficient bond, but Mephistopheles insists upon a contract signed in blood – for 'Blood is a very peculiar juice'. Faust is shown seated in his study, surrounded by all the accoutrements of a scholar, scientist and dabbler in the dark arts.

OPPOSITE: A twentieth-century illustration entitled *Faust and Mephistopheles*. Mephistopheles was another name for the Devil and, according to certain non-biblical texts, he was the second-in-command in hell, after Lucifer; he was the first to join with Lucifer in the rebellion against God during the war in heaven at the beginning of time. Harry Clark, the artist who created the illustrations for this 1925 edition of Goethe's play *Faust*, has given Mephistopheles an elastic form to emphasize the deceptiveness and ever-changing nature of the Devil – the literal 'shiftiness'of the Evil One. Faust is confronted by the tantalizing spectacle, conjured by Mephistopheles, of a half-naked woman.

ABOVE: This engraving was the second in the series of 29 plates made from drawings by Moritz Retzch, to illustrate an 1836 edition of Goethe's play *Faust*. Here, the artist shows Faust in the company of his servant Wagner being approached by Mephistopheles in the shape of a black dog; fire issues from the animal's paws. Only moments earlier, Faust had wanted to make contact with the spirit world. The next plate in the series will show the dog growing to an enormous size and being enveloped by a cloud, from which the diabolical Mephistopheles appears. Wagner had sagaciously advised his master, 'Do not call down that host of spirits, who fill the atmosphere like a stream and prepare a thousand dangers for man.' But his caution was to no avail.

ABOVE: The woman combing her hair and admiring herself in the mirror in this woodcut by German artist Albrecht Dürer sees only the posterior of the Devil in the glass. The theme was much reprised in medieval illustrations of the sin of Vanity, and was cut by the artist for a book of instruction for daughters first written in the fourteenth century. Although the traditional iconographic model of Pride and/or Vanity – a woman in thrall to her own image – was employed, the link between this sin and the road to hell has been made unusually graphic through the lurid depiction of the Devil and his bestial gesturing.

OPPOSITE: These hideous sword-wielding beasts are from a woodcut dating from 1510 by the German artist Hans Burgkmair the Elder. They represent the Seven Deadly Sins, with their scimitar-cum-banderols bearing the labels of the sins they personify. Hofart (Pride) is shown with the vestiges of a peacock's wings; Zorn is Wrath; Neid is Envy; Traghait is Sloth; Fressern is Gluttony; Unkeuschait is Avarice (in modern German the word denotes 'impurity'; and Begierde is Lust, with a dragon's shape. In truth, however, these imaginary creatures – half-mammalian, half-reptilian – are more or less interchangeable, their exaggerated monstrousness more a moralising illustration of the excess and exaggeration to which mortals are prone.

OPPOSITE: Antoine François Saint-Aubert, *Arrival at the Sabbat and Homage to the Devil*. This eighteenth-century painting shows how the fear of witches continued to haunt the popular imagination, even in the age of Enlightenment, although the witches here appear more phantasmagorical than terrifying. The aristocratic lady and her maidservant arrive at the Sabbat mounted on grotesque animals, while above them half-naked witches are borne through the air by a long-necked monster that recalls the dragon of the Apocalypse; warlocks (male witches) are recognizable by their horns and the pitchforks they carry. Another hideous, dragon-like monster bares its teeth in the foreground, in a ghastly, grimacing welcome.

ABOVE: This fire-and-brimstone painting of Don Giovanni being dragged into hell dates from 1796, although little is known about the life of its creator, the Italian artist Pietro Bini. A whole horde of bellowing, shrieking demons with monstrous heads and armed with cudgels, pitchforks and flays, has been summoned from the Inferno to drag the unrepentant sinner into its fiery depths. Those familiar with the opera *Don Giovanni* will know that its anti-hero has been confronted by the ghastly stone figure of the Commandant – here, in the guise of an equestrian statue – who has returned to consign the soul of the licentious nobleman Don Juan to the hellfire.

ABOVE: An illustration from a fifteenth-century French manuscript showing the temptation of the hermit saint Anthony the Great. Saint Anthony is shown engulfed by flames, a possible allusion to the fires of hell, and suffering temptations of the flesh in the shape of erotic visions, represented by the two women. That these clothed females are demonic in origin was made clear to the medieval reader by the devilish horns they sport; later portrayals of the temptations suffered by Saint Anthony in the desert would dispense with such outward signs of evil and focus instead on the female's tempting, naked flesh, with the saint gazing heavenward for spiritual help.

OPPOSITE: Lucas Cranach the Elder, *The Temptation of Saint Anthony*, 1506. In this nightmarish, frenzied vision of the demonic assaults suffered by the saint, unearthly stinging insects and flying beasts with beaks and pincers grapple with his form, tugging at and attaching themselves to every part of him, from head to toe – indeed, the hermit's face is barely distinguishable amid the bristling, crackling swarm. Cranach used an engraving by Martin Schöngauer (see Chapter 1, page 29), made some 30 years previously, as the basis for this drawing, but he added a tranquil Northern landscape. The gentle scene below the dense, battling mass only heightens the saint's torments, making his resistance all the more astonishing to behold.

OPPOSITE: The virtue of Humility ('Humilité') and the sin of Pride ('Orgeuil') – the father of all sins – are juxtaposed in the upper register of this page from the French illuminated manuscript, *La Somme Le Roy*, by Friar Laurent and an unknown illustrator, 1290–1300. Humility, perched on a stag, holds a flowering branch in her right hand, and a medallion (depicting a half-length female figure holding a palm and a book) in her left. Opposite, personifying Pride, is Ahaziah, king of Judah, shown falling from a battlemented building. Below left, a half-length figure of Christ appears from clouds to bless the sinner ('Le Pecheur'), while, below right, Christ, seated on the altar, shuns the hypocrite ('Hippocrite'), whose head is about to be seized by a smiling devil.

ABOVE: A woodcut from a 1473 German work entitled *Das Buch Belial*, by Jacobus de Teramo. It shows the demon Belial presenting King Solomon with a *grimoire* (a book that listed all the demons), with Moses behind him. *Das Buch Belial* essentially presented the 'case' for Christ and Satan, with Moses and Belial each arguing for their side. King Solomon appears in the biblical books of Kings, and it was during his reign that the Temple of Jerusalem was built. Although famed for his wisdom, in his later years he fell into idolatry. The ancient text known as the Testament of Solomon, a book not found in the Bible, describes the many demons whose help Solomon enlisted in the building of the Temple. Until the Middle Ages and beyond the narrative became a repository of magical lore about demons, detailing their individual spheres of influence, and how it was possible to thwart them.

BELOW: An early fourteenth-century illustration from *Le Breviari d'Amor* by the Provençal writer Matfré Ermengau. The scene illustrates the lure of worldly vanities, which here includes the outdoor and leisurely pursuits of hunting on horseback and hawking. The point, made by the clergy who preached against over-indulgence in such worldly pursuits, was that too-great-an attachment to the things 'of the world' and indulgence in pleasure turned the eyes of man away from God. By the Middle Ages, the concept of the Seven Deadly Sins had been well defined and mapped in pious works, thanks in part to the writings of the monk John Cassianus and to the sixth-century writings of Pope Gregory, one of the four Latin (Western) Fathers of the Church.

OPPOSITE (ABOVE): Temptation by way of personal adornment is depicted in this early fourteenth-century illustration, from *Le Breviari d'Amor* by Matfré Ermengau, as the Devil appearing to someone holding a mirror and a comb. One of the Seven Deadly Sins, Vanity and/or Pride (both *Superbia* in Latin, for the two were interchangeable in the Middle Ages) grew to be regarded as the worst of all sins, as it represented an inordinate love, and elevation, of the self. It was only with the Renaissance that Vanity, shown as a female nude admiring herself in a glass, would eclipse the broader notion of Pride, with its elevation of the self to a great height from which it can only fall.

OPPOSITE (BELOW): In this early fourteenth-century illustration from *Le Breviari d'Amor* by the troubadour poet Matfré Ermengau, temptation by way of pomp and banqueting is shown. The sin of Gluttony (*Gula*, in Latin) is made graver by the pomp and display that were a part of medieval banquets, and emphasizes its core meaning as a thoughtless waste of everything, including food. Gluttony – with Lust, a sin of the flesh – is depicted as a group of diners, including a crowned couple, seated around a table groaning with food and drink and surrounded by devils, some blowing trumpets, others apparently testing the blades of their knives to partake of the feast – or perhaps to punish the gluttons.

ABOVE: Eve hands Adam the apple in this painting by the Dutch master Hendrick Goltzius. Adam and Eve are shown reclining under the Tree of Knowledge in a luxuriant Garden of Eden. Painted as near life-size nudes, the pair could be mistaken for mythological lovers, were it not for the presence of the tempter snake – here, given a sweet female face to emphasize the deceptiveness of Satan – and Eve's knowing expression, belying the corruption that has taken place. Adam appears reluctant to share the apple, yet unable to resist the charms of Eve; he would rather be lost with her than saved without her (a theme Milton would later return to in *Paradise Lost*). The cat meets the viewer's gaze; the animal may here be a symbol of the Devil, for just as the cat lays traps to catch mice, so the Devil entraps the souls of sinners. It is also not by chance that two of the other animals depicted are goats, symbols of lust.

OPPOSITE: This nineteenth-century depiction of Good and Evil by the French painter Victor Orsel is today in the Musée des Beaux-Arts in Lyon, France. As the 'weaker sex' had been for centuries before, womankind is here the focus for the diverging paths of good and evil. The Archangel Michael protects the virtuous, saved woman, seen reading the Bible or a book of prayer, while the fallen woman – symbolically, in red, and with the book *Sapiente Liber* (*Book of Wisdom*) cast aside, at her feet – is claimed by the Devil, seen blasting a trumpet in her ear. Vignettes around the frame depict the rewards and punishments for the two ways, with the damned woman consigned to suffer (from bottom right, reading upwards) lust, rejection, the distress of the unmarried mother, and suicide in despair. It is an uncompromising message, rammed home by the tiny flying demons, the thorns, and the skull and crossbones.

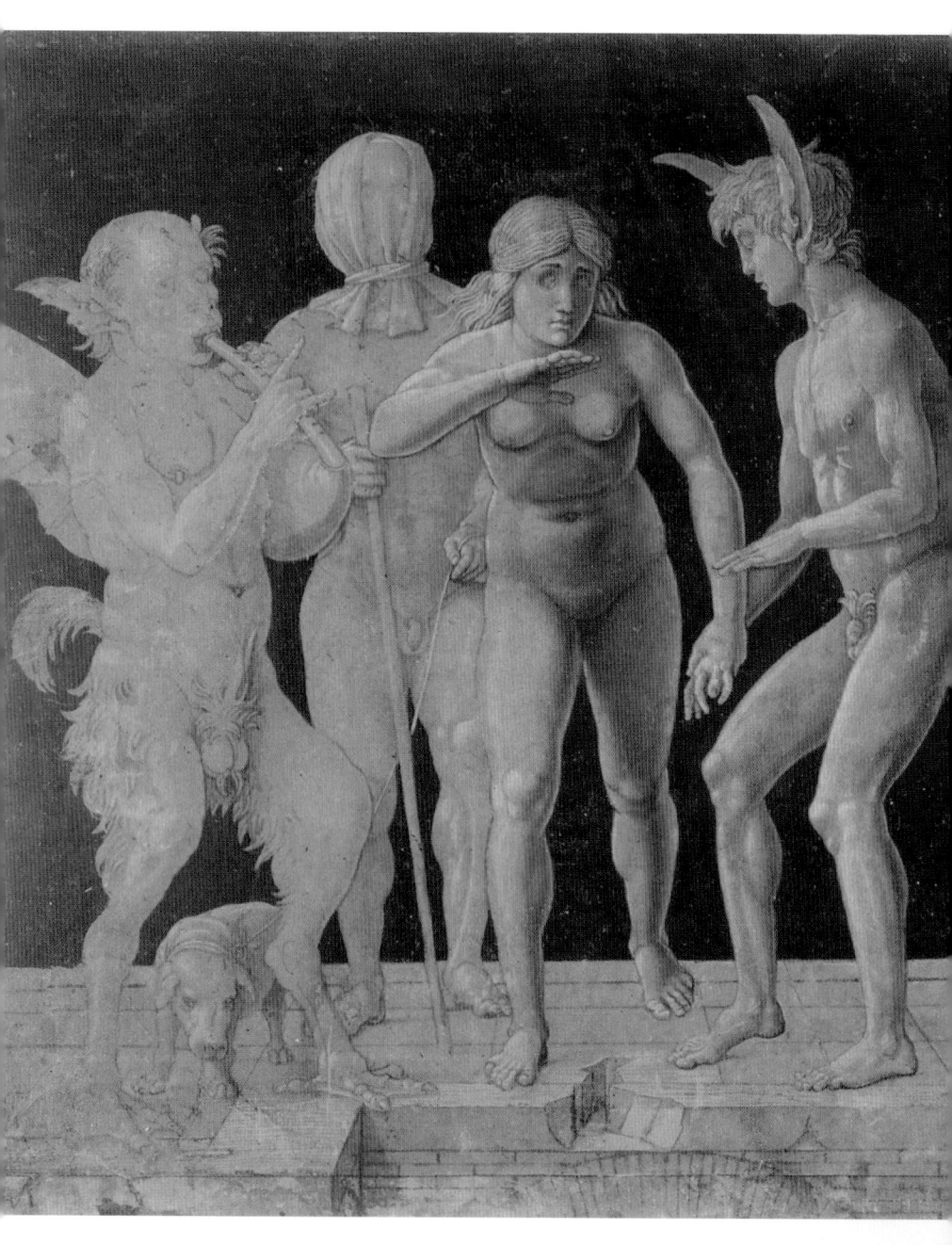

LEFT: This unfinished drawing (*c* 1490) by the Italian Renaissance artist Andrea Mantegna is an allegory of humanity in the grip of Ignorance. Entitled *Virtue in Flames*, it shows 'Error' as a man with ass's ears leading an unsuspecting woman who is both literally and morally blind. Error is encouraged by the winged figure of a satyr, symbolising Lust, with bat's wings and bird's feet, playing bagpipes. Meanwhile, Ignorance, a bloated woman, is served by Ingratitude and Avarice. The burning of laurel leaves, far right, implies that virtue and merit are literally going up in smoke in the domain of Ignorance. The original drawing (the bottom half is now lost) was a complete Allegory of Vice and Virtue. Steeped in classical learning, for Mantegna the sins of the early church had become rather more secular vices that were detrimental to the common good.

ABOVE: An illustration from *Le Fait des Romains*, a book produced in Bruges in 1479 for the English king Edward IV. In Roman literature Erichtho was a legendary and powerful sorceress. In the epic *Pharsalia* by the poet Lucan, the hideous, blood-thirsty Erichtho summoned the spirit of a dead soldier to reveal to Pompey the Great's son, Sextus Pompey, the outcome of the Battle of Pharsalus, which would force Pompey into exile. Erichtho also appears in Dante's *Divine Comedy*, where the author tells of the sorceress having compelled Virgil to descend into the realm of Pluto, god of the underworld, to retrieve a spirit. Edward was a renowned collector of manuscripts, and also patronized the new invention of printing.

OPPOSITE: A late fifteenth-century illustration of a scene from the classical tale of Orpheus and Eurydice, from a French translation of the Latin poet Ovid's *Metamorphoses*. Orpheus, with his lyre, is shown turning to glance at his wife, by this single act consigning her once more to the underworld. Horrible, bat-like demons are waiting to snatch her and transport her back there. Orpheus had descended into the underworld and succeeded, by the beauty of his music, in persuading Pluto – ruler of the dark realm – to let Eurydice follow him back to earth, so long as he did not look back at her. But at the last moment Orpheus turned to look at his wife, thereby breaking the condition under which she was to be restored to life.

ABOVE: This woodcut depiction) of the Devil surrounded by diminutive demons – or witches and sorcerers – had an ancient iconographic model in the form of classical depictions of satyrs and fauns, who were attendants to the god Bacchus (Dionysus, in the Greek pantheon). Satyrs had a human torso but the cloven hooves, hairy legs, pointed ears, beards and horns of a goat, and in this they resembled Bacchus, and also Pan, another of the god's retinue. Although they were not wholly negative creatures, their lascivious habits lent themselves readily to visual representations of the Devil. Bacchus might sport a wand tipped with a pine cone, an ancient fertility symbol; here, the Devil is carrying a torch, and presents a goat-like phallus. The sexual nature of Devil worship was much dwelt upon in popular tracts of the time.

RIGHT: A woodcut, depicting men and women dancing with the Devil, from the *Compendium Maleficarum*, 1608. This book, written by an Italian monk by the name of Francesco Maria Guazzo, was essentially a witch-hunters' manual for the early seventeenth century. Despite the rather comical-looking devil, and the seemingly – to modern eyes, at least – innocuous clothed women and men (actually witches and warlocks), the 'field guide' was taken seriously by Guazzo's contemporaries, being regarded as an authoritative companion to witchcraft and devil worship. Its author drew up a list of eleven headings under which witchcraft could be held to consist, which included a pact with the Devil, trampling on the Cross and asking Satan to take the candidate's name out of the book of Christ and inscribe it in his own diabolical book.

ABOVE: In another woodcut illustration from the *Compendium Maleficarum* (1608) the Devil is shown pronouncing a discourse to his crowd of followers, comprised of warlocks and witches, who gather round him, listening eagerly to his 'sermon'. The Devil is raised up on a dais, with a canopy over his head, enthroned in the manner of a king. The style of Guazzo's book was more popular than academic, and it gave many 'examples' of the signs of sorcery, thus paying homage to superstitions of the worst kind. Its listing of witches' 'crimes' included killing their own infants and eating their flesh, poisonings, and causing disease in cattle. However, such 'evidence' tended to be based on confessions extracted from the suspected sorcerers under torture.

ABOVE: Andrea del Castagno, *The Last Supper, c* 1447, fresco in the refectory of Santa Appollonia, Florence. This detail from the fresco shows the apostle Judas Iscariot who betrayed Jesus for 30 pieces of silver, and thus set in motion the forces that led to the Crucifixion. He is seated in a solitary position, on the opposite side of the table from Christ and the other Apostles, making him readily identifiable. Even so, there is no mistaking this Judas – Castagno has given him a swarthy complexion, dark hair and a thick goatish beard, with pointed ears and a long, hooked nose. Unlike the other Apostles, he has no halo. Judas exemplified the Devil's method of leading men into wicked ways, for the Gospels make clear that the Devil entered into Judas when he decided to deliver the Messiah to the Sanhedrin, the chief judicial council of the Jews.

OPPOSITE: Page from an illuminated manuscript entitled *La Somme Le Roy*, which was produced in France between 1290 and 1300; its author was Friar Laurent, but the artist behind the beautiful, intricately painted illuminations is not known. The upper register personifies Mercy (left) and Avarice (right). Avarice is shown as a ragged, bearded miser transferring gold coins from a pot into a large chest, in which task he is assisted by three eager devils. Mercy, on the other hand, is a crowned figure, holding a medallion with a dove, and who offers a garment to a poor, half-naked man. Below left, Abraham is shown with the three angels, while below right, the biblical story, in Kings, of the widow's oil (whereby the empty jars miraculously filled with oil), is illustrated – contrasting this reward for godliness with the godless act of hoarding.

ABOVE: A colour print by the Victorian illustrator Arthur Rackham from a 1915 edition of Charles Dickens' *A Christmas Carol*. The theme of the Devil as tempter is here horribly apparent in the crooked, claw-like finger of the Devil, beckoning Scrooge who clutches his moneybags. The form here is that of the Devil in the modern imagination – cloven hoofed, with hairy legs, horns and a pointed tail (in fact, the very image of a satyr).

ABOVE: A scene from the series of illustrations depicting Infernal Punishments for the Seven Deadly Sins that appeared in a 1523 edition of *Le Grant Kalendrier et Compost des Bergiers* by Nicolas Le Rouge. Dating from 1496 and originally printed in the French city of Troyes, it was France's first almanac. The book contained a mixture of astrological and scientific information, practical advice, and moral instruction on how to conduct oneself in this life so as to attain Paradise in the next. Such was its success that there were at least 40 editions of the book. In this illustration, those guilty of the sin of Pride are being punished in hell by beaked and horned demons – the punishment for this most terrible of sins (which, after all, was what sparked the fall of Lucifer from heaven) was to be broken on a wheel.

Monsters and Grotesques

From the Blemmyae (with his face on his chest) and the Sciopod (with his one, giant, foot) of the bestiaries that became popular in the twelfth-century to the unearthly hybrids that feature in the work of artists such as Hieronymus Bosch, medieval art seethes with depictions of monsters and grotesques.

Whether among the illiterate majority, looking up at the façade of one of the great gothic cathedrals, or one of the fortunate elite, wealthy enough to own a prized Bestiary, Psalter, Book of Hours or *Bible Moralisée* ('moralised' or allegorised Bible), every Christian would have been confronted by images of the strange and monstrous in daily life, particularly from the twelfth century when there was an upsurge in artistic interest in portrayals of Satan and his cohorts and in monsters. Whether carved in stone or painstakingly depicted in books, wall-paintings, pictures or glass, such images served as a constant visual reminder both of the wonders of God's wider creation and of the moral and physical perils that lay in wait for the Christian who strayed from the true spiritual Path, or who ventured beyond the frontiers of the known Christian world.

Some of the monsters – for example, the dog-headed cynocephali or the man-eating hybrid, the manticore, as featured in works such as the eighth-century *Liber Monstrorum* (Book of Monsters) and the tenth-century *Marvels of the East* – were largely based on the ideas of Classical authors, including Homer, the Greek historian Herodotus and the Roman historian Pliny the Elder (23–79 AD). As important as a sourcebook for medieval artists and writers as Pliny's *Natural History* was the *Physiologus*, probably written in Alexandria in the third or fourth century. Other monsters were inspired by Biblical descriptions, for example Leviathan (referred to in Job and Isaiah and the Psalms; it was common to depict the entrance to hell as Leviathan's mouth); some were based on real creatures that travellers may have seen, and whose descriptions were embellished in the retelling; yet others stood as symbols for ideas in which medieval Christians believed devoutly, whether or not they believed that monsters existed in the physical world.

By definition, monsters are 'ugly as sin' and the saying points to the role played by monstrous creatures in the medieval world view. Medieval Christians believed that God had arranged the natural world so as to provide a source of instruction to humanity; they also believed that outward form reflected the inner moral state. That is, physical ugliness, imperfection or 'otherness' was generally – though not always – equated with moral imperfection, with sinfulness. Thus monsters and grotesques could act as moral allegories, both warning Christians of the consequences of sin and reminding them of the spiritual battle every Christian was obliged to wage in his or her daily life against the forces of evil, in personal spiritual terms and in the wider world.

Ironically, in their depictions of monsters it is clear that the craftsmen and artists who created them brought an ingenuity and imaginative vigour to their work that was often lacking in images of angels. For while in the latter the artist had to evoke the angels' serenity and non-carnal nature, with monsters and demons the artist had a far greater degree of creative freedom; he could allow his imagination to run free in portraying the monsters' chaotic, noisy restlessness and carnality.

OPPOSITE: Hell; detail of a painting (*c* 1550) by the 'JS monogrammist' in the Doges Palace, Venice, Italy. Just as for Hieronymus Bosch's hideous hybrid creatures, the sources for the unnamed artist's unusual images – the turtle with the human face and pince-nez, the duck-like creature and the demonic dragonfly – were the dark corners of the medieval imagination, the monsters and gargoyles of cathedral decoration, and the illustrations in bestiaries. Here, however, such creatures are given a sharply personal twist, and their ranks boosted by crackling beetles and slithering snakes and snails. The picture teems with demonic activity, as they torment and dismember the tiny human figures cast into hell.

ABOVE: Detail of the right-hand panel of Hieronymus Bosch's (*c* 1450–1516) triptych, *The Garden of Earthly Delights* (*c* 1500, Prado, Madrid, Spain). The left-hand panel of Bosch's triptych depicts Paradise, the central panel shows postlapsarian humankind on the eve of the flood and the right-hand panel shows hell. Many critics, however, believe that the panels do not present a simple, continuous tale of decline and fall and, certainly, the hell shown in the right-hand panel is no more conventional than the implicitly compromised Paradise of the first panel. Bosch's hell, for example, is not entered via Leviathan's mouth nor are there traditional demons herding the judged into the flames of eternal damnation. Rather, the action appears to be taking place on this earth. Armies fight and cities burn in the top part of the panel; those who escape across the ice and water in the middle part to reach the dry land shown in the bottom third are either tortured, or crushed, by musical instruments, or are devoured by one of Bosch's strange hybrid creatures, like the demonic bird-headed creature shown here. Wearing a crown fashioned from a cauldron, it sits on a throne-like toilet and excretes a translucent egg containing helpless humans: together these plunge towards the cesspit below.

ABOVE: The head of Quetzalcoatl, the Plumed Serpent, on the side of the pyramid temple at Teotihuacan, Mexico. The temple, which was constructed between AD 150 and 300, is dedicated to both Quetzalcoatl, the Aztec god of night and all material things, and, possibly, to Tlaloc, the rain god (the latter is disputed by scholars). The serpent was important in Mesoamerican religions from as early as 1150 BC as a representation of the fertility of the earth. But it was in Teotihuacan, in about 150 BC, that the attributes of the god were increased; this development was symbolized by the snake's acquisition of the feathers of the Quetzal, a brilliantly plumed native bird. Subsequently, Quetzalcoatl acquired the attributes of other Mesoamerican gods and, eventually, under the Toltec's dualistic belief-system, he was transformed into one of the gods of the creation. The Aztecs later attributed the creation of the world to Tezcatlipoca, the Aztec god of night, and Quetzalcoatl, who were opposite and equal.

OPPOSITE (BELOW): The damned being swallowed up by the jaws of hell – represented by the mouth of the sea-monster Leviathan – as depicted on a roof-boss in the nave of Norwich Cathedral, England. Completed in 1145, Norwich Cathedral has over 1,000 roof bosses; some illustrate biblical scenes or point up moral lessons, as here. Others show a range of beasts and monsters. From the thirteenth century in particular, the carvings (on general stonework, as well as bosses) of the great cathedrals often acted as a kind of encyclopedia of the knowledge of the time, showing examples of all the then-known animals, whether real or legendary.

RIGHT: Clay mask of the Assyro-Babylonian monster Huwawa (Humbaba or Khumbaba in some texts), from Sippar, southern Iraq, c 1800–1600 BC. Sippar was one of the most important cult centres for the powerful sun-god, Shamash. As well as being the upholder of justice and law, Shamash was the god of divination and Sippar was particularly associated with the practice of what was seen as the science of divination. Masks such as this were used in divination ceremonies. A favourite method for predicting the future in ancient Mesopotamia was to study the shape and colour of the internal organs of a sacrificed animal (often a sheep or lamb); when examining the animal's entrails the expert divination priests would cross-refer to a 'library' of clay masks such as this to help them make their analysis or analyses. A cuneiform inscription on the back intestines were found to be in the shape of Huwawa's face (as represented by this mask), such an omen would mean 'revolution'.

OPPOSITE: Varaha rescues the earth from Hiranyaksha; an illustration by an unknown artist from the Pahari region, North India, *c* 1740. The four-armed Varaha is shown holding objects characteristic of Vishnu, the discus, a conch shell, a lotus and a club with which he strikes the sea-demon Hiranyaksha. Hiranyaksha had earlier taken the earth – represented by the earth-goddess Bhu in Hindu mythology – to the depths of the ocean; here, Varaha has rescued the earth/earth-goddess (symbolized by the small landscape) from the swirling black depths and balances her on his tusks. Blood pours from the demon's chest and he staggers back, dropping his broken sword. In most illustrations of this myth Bhu is depicted in female form. The boar Varaha, meanwhile, is Vishnu appearing in the third of his ten incarnations (avatara).

ABOVE: A depiction of Ravana's Golden Palace. A Hindu demon-king with 20 arms and ten heads, Ravana was chief of the Rakshasas, creatures with magical powers who were fated to sow discord in peoples' lives. Ravana gains great wealth and power through his conquests across India, but becomes corrupt. The *Ramayana* tells of how Rama (Vishnu in human form) attacks Ravana, who has abducted Rama's wife, Sita, in his stronghold at Lanka. Eventually, using arrows with magical powers, Rama succeeds in killing Ravana, an act which represents the triumph of good over evil. Here, Ravana is at the centre of the picture, while the battle takes place around him.

OPPOSITE (ABOVE): A manticore, or mantichora, as illustrated in Edward Topsell's *The History of Four-footed Beasts*, published in 1607. Topsell's work attempted to summarize all the real and mythical zoological knowledge collected since antiquity. He relied particularly on Conrad Gesner (1516–65) and his *Historiae animalium*, which had been published in 1551. Gesner probably referred in turn to classical sources: the creature had been described by the Greek traveller Ctesias and, later, by Pliny. Topsell noted that 'This beast or Monster … is bred amongst the Indians, having a treble row of teeth beneath and above, whose greatness, roughness, and feet are like a Lyons, his face and ears are like a mans, his eyes gray, and colour red, his tail like the tail of a scorpion, of the earth, armed with a sting, casting forth sharp pointed quills … his appetite is especially to the flesh of men.' The mantichora was said to live in the depths of the earth and to have a mellifluous voice, which it supposedly used to confuse its victims before devouring them; all attributes that led it to be seen as the embodiment of evil.

OPPOSITE (BELOW): Another depiction of a manticore, from an unnamed medieval bestiary. This version of the legendary man-eating creature has goat-like horns and forequarters. In his *The Dictionary of Mysticism and the Occult*, Nevill Drury notes that the manticore 'took its name from the Persian *mardkhara*, a man-eating tiger'. Compilers of medieval bestiaries borrowed details from earlier sources, and characteristics of legendary animals such as the manticore were embellished or modified in the process. The authors of the Medieval Bestiary website, for example, comment that Isidore of Seville's *Etymologies* was extensively used by later compilers of the bestiaries (Isidore was born early in the second half of the sixth century and died in about AD 636), but that Isidore himself 'took much of his information from Aristotle and Pliny, who also wrote about real and imaginary animals. Isidore, as usual, accepted whatever his sources told him; observation of the real world has little part in his 'zoology'. However, unlike the earlier *Physiologus*, Isidore did not include any moralisations or allegory in his beast stories. The compilers of the later bestiaries quoted Isidore extensively and added the allegory Isidore left out.

ABOVE: An ivory figure of a griffin-headed demon from Toprakkale in eastern Anatolia (modern Turkey), eighth–seventh century BC. Ivory carvings were widely used to decorate important pieces of furniture in antiquity and it is believed that this example may have been part of a throne. Griffin-headed demons were protective deities, and it would have been included here because of the divine protection it was thought to give to the throne's occupant. While similar creatures are depicted on Assyrian wall reliefs at Nimrud, this carving comes from Toprakkale in Urartu. This fortified citadel contained a major temple of the god Haldi. Urartu had disappeared by about 600 BC, possibly destroyed by the raids of horse-borne warriors, known to the Greeks as Scythians.

ABOVE: Demons drag the souls of the damned into Leviathan's mouth; an illustration from a German broadsheet of *c* 1530. It became popular from about the twelfth century to portray the entrance to hell as the sea-monster Leviathan's mouth; the symbolism was derived from biblical references to Leviathan, for example, in the Book of Job (41:19: 'Out of his mouth go burning lamps, and sparks of fire leap out') and Revelation (11:7), where the narrator speaks of 'the beast that ascendeth out of the bottomless pit'. Sometimes a cauldron is placed in Leviathan's mouth – an image which is also derived from Job (41:20: 'Out of his nostrils goeth smoke, as out of a seething pot or caldron').

LEFT: Francisco de Goya, *The Colossus*, 1808–12 (sometimes called *Panic*). In Goya's enigmatic painting, a swarthy, naked giant strides across the landscape. Streams of humans, with their wagons and cattle – all mere ants in comparison – pour this way and that across the lower part of the composition, fleeing in panic. The giant, and the demonic energy he embodies, may symbolize war, chaos, the force of evil or the sheer crushing strength of Napoleon's army. Certainly, the monstrous being highlights one of the recurring motifs of Goya's work – that power will inevitably be used to despoil or destroy.

OPPOSITE (ABOVE): A detail from the funerary papyrus of Taminiu. The papyrus dates from the Third Intermediate Period, *c* 950 BC and is from Thebes in Egypt. Here, the deceased Taminiu is seen receiving water from Nut, who appears as a sycamore goddess. In ancient Egyptian belief, demons were among the many obstacles encountered on the path to the Afterlife. Funerary books were created to assist the deceased on the journey, and contained the spells needed to overcome each problem. Underworld demons guarded the gates to the Mansion of Osiris, where the dead were judged. The demons were often depicted, as here, in a mummified form, crouching and holding sharp knives. Most had the heads of recognizable animals while others, such as the double snake-headed demon in the top row, were creatures of fantasy. The upright snake, with human arms and legs, was the demon guardian who stood at the doorway of the judgement chamber.

OPPOSITE (BELOW): The Egyptian goddess Bast, shown in the form of a cat, killing the demon Apep. From a lithographic copy of the Papyrus of Hunefer, Eighteenth Dynasty (*c* 1370 BC). Bast was a local goddess of Lower Egypt until about 950 BC, when she became one of the great national divinities; her popularity was at its greatest in the fourth century BC. As the cat was her sacred animal, she was often represented as a cat-headed woman. Along with the powerful Set and others, Bast aided the great Sun-god Ra on his journey through the underworld each night, during which Ra would be attacked by the evil Apep (who was represented by a great snake or serpent, as he is here), whose aim it was to prevent Ra, his eternal enemy, from rising again in the morning.

ABOVE: A Hippopotamus-headed figure from Egypt. This figure dates from the end of the Eighteenth Dynasty (*c* 1325 BC) and is today held in the British Museum, London, England. The lower part of the body is human, and is shown crouching and mummified; this is the typical form that the demon guardians of the underworld take. Ancient Egyptians saw the hippopotamus as a dangerous creature. However, although the male was frequently associated with chaos – often in the form of the god Seth, who murdered Osiris in an attempt to seize the throne of Egypt – the animal's dangerous power could also be used for the benefit of the dead, assisting them on their journey to the afterlife. This figure, from a royal tomb in the Valley of the Kings, Thebes, served precisely this purpose, being one of several provided for the king by the god Osiris to assist him on his final journey.

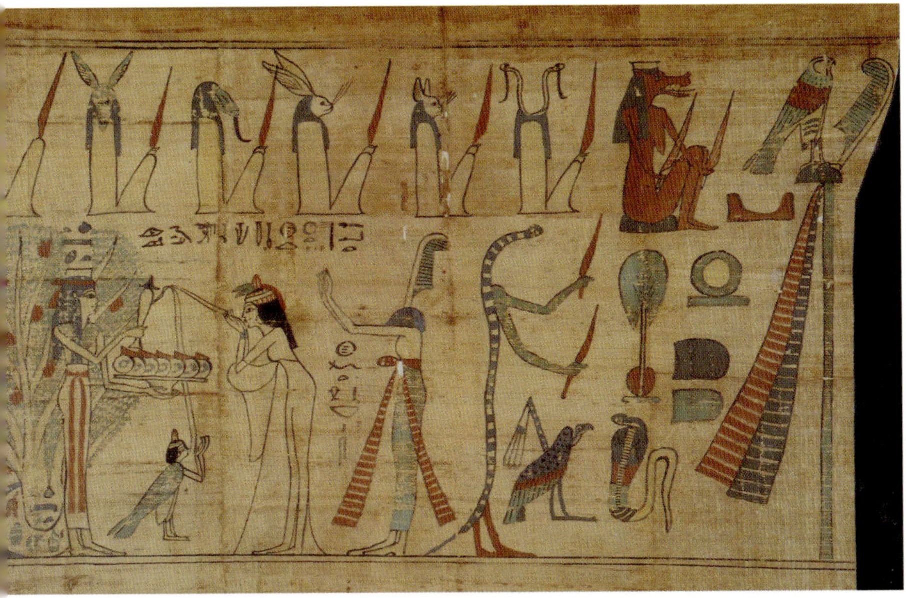

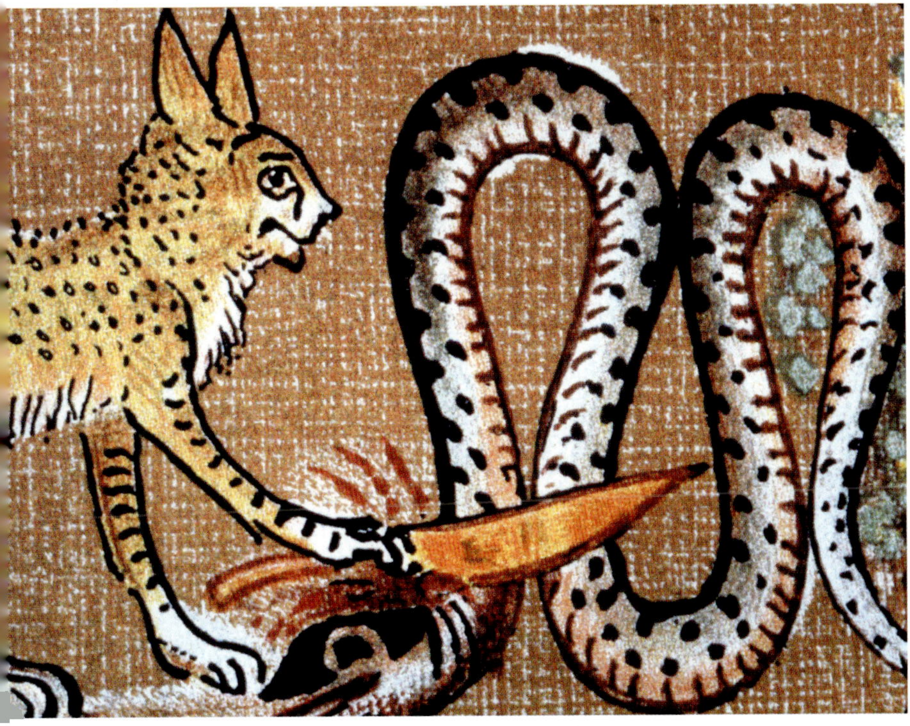

ABOVE: A whale; a miniature from an English bestiary of the twelfth century. Bestiaries became popular in the twelfth century, particularly in England and France. There were two main types: the first, with its descriptions of both real and legendary animals, beasts, birds and even plants, was a kind of medieval encyclopedia of natural history; while the second described the animal and ascribed it a symbolic meaning to teach the reader a moral lesson, as here. Both drew on the *Physiologus*, an early and influential type of bestiary probably written between the second and fourth centuries. The author of the *Physiologus* equates the whale with the Devil; it draws in the small fish (representing those who are weak in faith) but casts no spell over those whose faith is strong – as is the case with Jonah, who is 'vomited out … upon the dry land' (2:10) by the whale once he has 'remembered the Lord' (Jonah 2:7). In this illustration the whale signifies the Devil and the ship the world, with its cargo of humans.

ABOVE: Fish and mythical creatures, from a thirteenth-century bestiary and herbarium. This image probably opened the section of the book of beasts usually entitled 'the swimmers'. The fish are a fairly unusual inclusion in such a text, which is usually dominated by mammals. Among the fish swims a spectacular sea horse. The horned creature in the lower left of the image may well represent the 'hydrus' or Nile monitor, an underwater lizard which climbs inside the mouth of a sleeping crocodile and eats it alive from within. In symbolic terms, the crocodile represents hell and the hydrus, Christ: Christ enters hell to save the souls trapped there.

ABOVE: In Maurice Garçon's *La Vie Execrable de Guillemette Babin* (c 1560), Satan is presented as presiding at the Sabbat, attended by demons. The throned devil is shown in satyr form with ram's horns, cloven foot and a serpent's tail. Notice also the occultist trappings on display, such as the orb, pentagrams and trident.

OPPOSITE: Albrecht Dürer (1471–1528) was a supremely gifted German Renaissance artist who revolutionized woodcut printmaking. This animated and animalistic bat-winged demon exhibits Dürer's fascination with the Gothic period, particularly in the profusion of intricate linear traceries and the macabre subject matter.

OPPOSITE: A sea monster; pencil sketch by the British artist Gordon Wain, 1990. Both the Bible and Christian iconography make extensive use of the whale, or sea-monster, as an allegory for the Devil, or for untamed, chaotic (and implicitly pagan) forces. In the Old Testament, Isaiah refers to the coming punishment of 'leviathan, that crooked serpent; and [the Lord] shall slay the dragon that is in the sea' (27:1), while in Job, the Lord talks of Leviathan, the 'king over all the children of pride' who 'maketh the deep to boil like a pot … Upon earth there is not his like, who is made without fear' (41:31–34); and in Jonah, as mentioned elsewhere, the Lord prepares 'a great fish to swallow up Jonah' (1:17) because he has fled from His presence. In the New Testament, Matthew uses Jonah's experience as an allegory for Christ's descent into hell ('For as Jonas was three days and three nights in the whale's belly; so shall the Son of man be three days and three nights in the heart of the earth' (12:40), while in Revelation (13:1–10) a beast 'rise[s] up out of the sea, having seven heads and ten horns'. Meanwhile, in paintings of Last Judgement scenes (again, as noted elsewhere), the entrance to hell is often portrayed as Leviathan's mouth.

ABOVE: A sea-demon, from Ambroise Paré's *Des Monstres et Prodiges* (first published in 1573; the illustration is from a book of Paré's complete works, published in 1840). By the late sixteenth century, the interest in monsters and grotesques had certainly not diminished, but there had been a change in tone, as exemplified by the work of Paré, a leading French surgeon who pioneered the development of new surgical techniques. In his *Des Monstres*, Paré searches for natural explanations for deformity, rather than assuming they are the result of sin or moral laxity or association with the Devil and seeing them as a demonstration of God's judgement on wrongdoers. The explanations Paré offered were not 'scientific' or 'rational' in the sense that those terms are understood today – but his and similar works of the time marked a significant change in approach in looking for explanations in the natural, rather than in the supernatural, world.

ABOVE: Gargoyles of a griffin (left), a vulture (right) and a one-horned demon on the roof of the Cathedral of Notre Dame, Paris, France. Work on the cathedral began in 1163; and was largely complete by 1267. In contemporary bestiaries, the griffin (also spelled griffon or gryphon) and vulture had complex and often ambiguous allegorical meanings. For example, in the Aberdeen Bestiary (written around 1200), the vulture is described both as a symbol of Christ (as both descend to earth on seeing death and, like Christ, the vulture often dies when making the descent: it gives up its life in coming to earth) and of evil (the vulture follows armies, as it knows the battle to come will yield corpses for it to feed on, just as the Devil follows sin, as it will yield souls for hell). The griffin – part eagle, part lion – is even more complex as a symbol, having the best and worst qualities of both creatures. The lion and eagle are noble, have great strength and are the kings of the animal world; yet, like the Devil, they are also ferocious and merciless and feed on those weaker than themselves.

OPPOSITE: A demon carved on a fifteenth-century bench-end in Saint Mary's Church, Woolpit, Suffolk, England. Other bench-ends in the church feature beautifully carved birds, dogs (including one with a rabbit in its mouth and one holding a duck) and what may be a cat with a rat. Many of the bench-ends, however, are carved in the form of creatures that the carpenter, or carpenters, were unlikely to have seen in real life (though they may have seen printed woodcut illustrations of them): a pair of ibex, and a lion, for example. Whatever the inspiration for the carvings, members of the congregation would have been aware that some had allegorical meanings – and that others had been carved simply in a spirit of fun. One bench-end, in the shape of a monkey in a friar's habit, falls into both categories: it plays on the allegorical meaning of the monkey (it was a symbol of foolishness and vanity) to poke fun at the friar.

OPPOSITE: A detail of Tyrannia from *Il Mattino Governo* (Allegory of Bad Government), a fresco by Ambrogio Lorenzetti (*c* 1293–1348) in the Sala della Pace in the Palazzo Pubblico, Siena, Italy. The Allegory of Bad Government is situated on the wall opposite the Allegory of Good Government. In the central band of the latter, Siena (represented by a man sitting on a throne) is surrounded by six crowned female figures representing the virtues of good government – Peace, Fortitude, Prudence, Magnanimity, Temperance and Justice. Above them, in the upper band representing the heavenly sphere, Wisdom (holding a Bible and a pair of scales) floats against a blue sky. In the lower band, councillors and citizens gather while, on the longer wall, scenes of Siena show the citizens calmly going about their daily lives: working, talking and repairing houses in the town, and hunting and harvesting in the well-tended countryside. On the opposite wall, the demonic Tyrannia dominates the scene: richly dressed and with a gold cup in her hand, she is surrounded by the Vices (including a satyr) and a goat – symbol of lust – sits at her feet. Below her, Justitia sits disconsolately, her scales broken. Scenes of the town and countryside show death, destruction and ruin.

ABOVE: The 'demon king' Maymon (a corruption of Mammon) from an English grimoire, *c* 1500. Grimoires – books of magical knowledge and instruction – appeared from the late Middle Ages. One of the first, the *Key of Solomon*, was possibly written in the thirteenth century and this in turn may have inspired works such as *The Lesser Key of Solomon* (also called the *Lemegeton*) and Johann Weyer's *De Praestigiis Daemonum et Incantationibus ac Venificiis* (On the *Illusions of the Demons and on Spells and Poisons*), which was published in 1563. Weyer's *Pseudomonarchia Daemonum* (*Hierarchy of Demons*) was first published as an appendix to *De Praestigiis Daemonum*, and later as a separate book in 1677. Each of these – except for the *Key of Solomon*, which does not mention any of the 72 spirits listed in the *Pseudomonarchia Daemonum* – contains descriptions of the hierarchy of demons and gives instructions to the reader both on how to summon them up and how to protect oneself from them. The number and hierarchy of the featured demons, together with their characteristics, differ somewhat in each individual book. The figure of Mammon features in neither the *Lemegeton* nor in Weyer's *Pseudomonarchia Daemonum*, but in his 1589 *De Confessionibus Maleficorum et Sagarum* (*The Confession of Warlocks and Witches*), Peter Binsfeld established an explicit association between Mammon as a powerful demon and the deadly sin of avarice or greed, echoing the twelfth-century theologian Peter Lombard, who wrote that 'Riches are called by the name of a devil, namely Mammon, for Mammon is the name of a devil'.

ABOVE: An elephant battles with a dragon; an illustration from a thirteenth-century French bestiary. The dragon – symbol of Satan – was seen as the traditional enemy of the elephant and images of the two fighting were popular in bestiaries; here, although the dragon tears the elephant's flesh with its tail and jaws, the elephant is in the ascendant. In allegorical terms, the small elephant was seen as a type of Christ, while the adult male elephant and its mate symbolized Adam and Eve: by legend, elephants were reluctant to mate (and thus symbolically, they were seen as living in a state of prelapsarian innocence) but the dragon/snake seduced them into doing so; after their 'Fall', the small elephant is born to redeem them. Also, because the burning skin of the elephant was by legend reputed to drive away snakes, the elephant was used as a symbol of the power of God's commandments, which drive evil from man's soul.

OPPOSITE: Behemoth and Leviathan, an engraving from William Blake's *Illustrations of the Book of Job*, 1826. God (top), with his left hand, points down towards the hippopotamus-like Behemoth, the land beast, and Leviathan, depicted as a dragon-like sea beast. He instructs Job (centre, under the Lord), whose faith he is testing, about the extent and power of His creation (in the Old Testament book of Job 40:15, the Lord says to Job, 'Behold now behemoth, which I made with thee'; and in 40:19 Behemoth is described to Job as 'the chief of the ways of God; he that made him can make his sword to approach unto him'). Leviathan – symbol of Satan and described by Isaiah as the 'crooked serpent' – is, in Job 41:34 described as 'a king over all the children of pride'. In his book *Jerusalem* Blake used the two monsters as symbols of war by land and by sea. Here, the Lord is pointing out to Job the negativeness of his faith so far; for, contained within a globe-like sphere, these terrible beasts are – like the other Wonders of his Creation – all of his creating.

LEFT: Adam and Eve caught in the coils of serpents; a detail from the Gothic part of the west front of Lincoln cathedral, Lincoln, England. Here, Adam and Eve are in the act of helping each other eat the fruit (shown here as figs) of the Tree of the Knowledge of Good and Evil, although in the book of Genesis Eve eats first and then offers the fruit to Adam. Both are smiling and, it seems, are unaware of their nakedness: this is their last moment of innocence, before their Fall into the knowledge of good and evil, and awareness of their sexuality. The latter is emphasized by the positioning of the heads of each of the serpents – between the buttocks of each; from here, the serpents peer towards Adam and Eve, as if they are waiting in anticipation for them to become aware of what they have done. In the sinuous movement of the serpents that curl around Adam and Eve, the stonemason evokes the coils of sexuality that will soon bind the two.

OPPOSITE (ABOVE): A gargoyle in the shape of a demon's head, the Church of Saint Thomas the Martyr, Winchelsea, Sussex, England. The wide staring eyes and the open contorted mouth with its vividly protruding tongue make it appear as if the demon is screaming. As well as evoking the sounds of hell, the open mouth, over-large tongue and satyr-like pointed ears of the gargoyle also emphasize the Devil's carnal nature, reminding the observer that Satan was associated with rampant sexuality. Ironically, because angels were ethereal beings associated with stillness, harmony and peace, stonemasons had far less creative leeway when sculpting images of them: while angels had to be almost static and androgynous in appearance (to evoke their peacefulness and non-corporeality), when carving devils and demons the stonemasons could let their imaginations run free.

OPPOSITE (BELOW): Beaked demons on the west front of Lincoln Cathedral, Lincoln, England. The Cathedral as it exists today is the third to occupy the site. The first, commissioned by William the Conqueror in 1072, was badly damaged by fire in about 1142; the second collapsed in 1185; the third was started in 1192 and was more or less completed about 100 years later, although the building as it is today was not finished until the fifteenth century. The remains of part of the original Norman west end – including the stone carvings seen here – were incorporated into the Gothic west front during the thirteenth-century rebuilding. These carved demons reflect the severity of the original, fortress-like structure, one purpose of which was to demonstrate the power of the new Norman rulers: for these demons are cold, stern, silent, watchful, distant – almost sentry-like – unlike the agitated, writhing, physically contorted demons of the Gothic era.

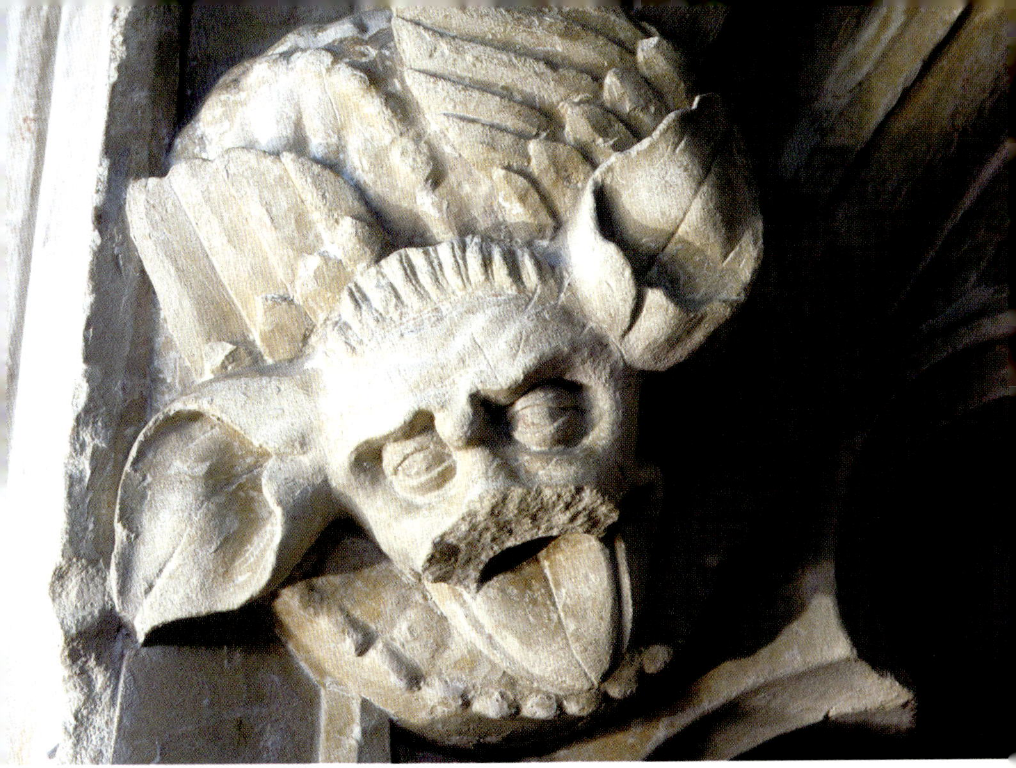

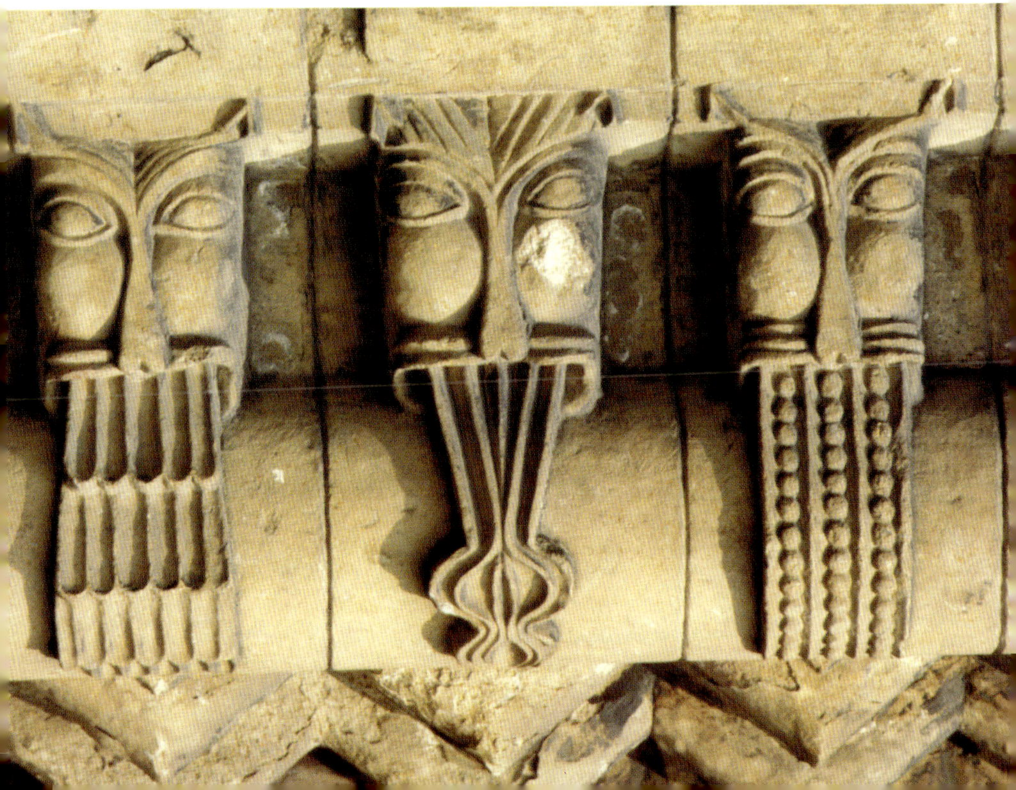

OPPOSITE: A selection of monstrous human races; a hand-coloured woodcut illustration of 1449, copied from Konrad von Megenberg's *Das Buch der Natur* (*The Book of Nature*), which was written in the mid-fourteenth century. Among the races shown are: an Abarimon (top row right), who were reputed to be fast runners, even though their feet pointed backwards; a Cynocephalus (centre row, left), a dog-headed race who were supposed to communicate by barking and who, in the later Middle Ages, came to represent unconverted pagans; an Epiphagus (centre row, middle left), with his eyes in his shoulders; a Sciopod (centre row, middle right) who used his one large foot as shelter; and a Cyclope or Arimaspi (bottom row, left). From Bavaria, Konrad von Megenberg (1309–74) was a leading scholar and writer; *Das Buch der Natur*, his best-known work, was the first encyclopedia of natural history to be written in the German language. As well as summarizing established knowledge in areas ranging from anatomy and astronomy to zoology, it also contained a section describing the monstrous human races that were then believed to live in the East.

ABOVE: Alexander the Great encounters a group of Blemmyae, headless human creatures with their faces on their chests; from a French translation of the Alexander Romance made in Rouen before *c* 1445. The manuscript was presented to Margaret of Anjou, wife of King Henry VI of England, by the Earl of Shrewsbury. Alexander become king of Macedon and of most of mainland Greece in 336 BC; a military genius, he conquered the Persian Empire, founded Alexandria with its magnificent library, and led his troops into northern India, eventually overrunning the Punjab. He died in 323 BC, having spread Hellenism throughout the Near East. Over the succeeding centuries, Alexander's feats were embellished, adapted and varied to create a body of legends that reflected, in turn, the beliefs and concerns of the particular writer-compiler. For example in some collections of the twelfth and thirteenth centuries, Alexander began to be cast as a model of Christian knightly chivalry; as in this later illuminated translation, where he is shown bravely encountering the pagan Monstrous Races to be found in the dark, unexplored regions of the world.

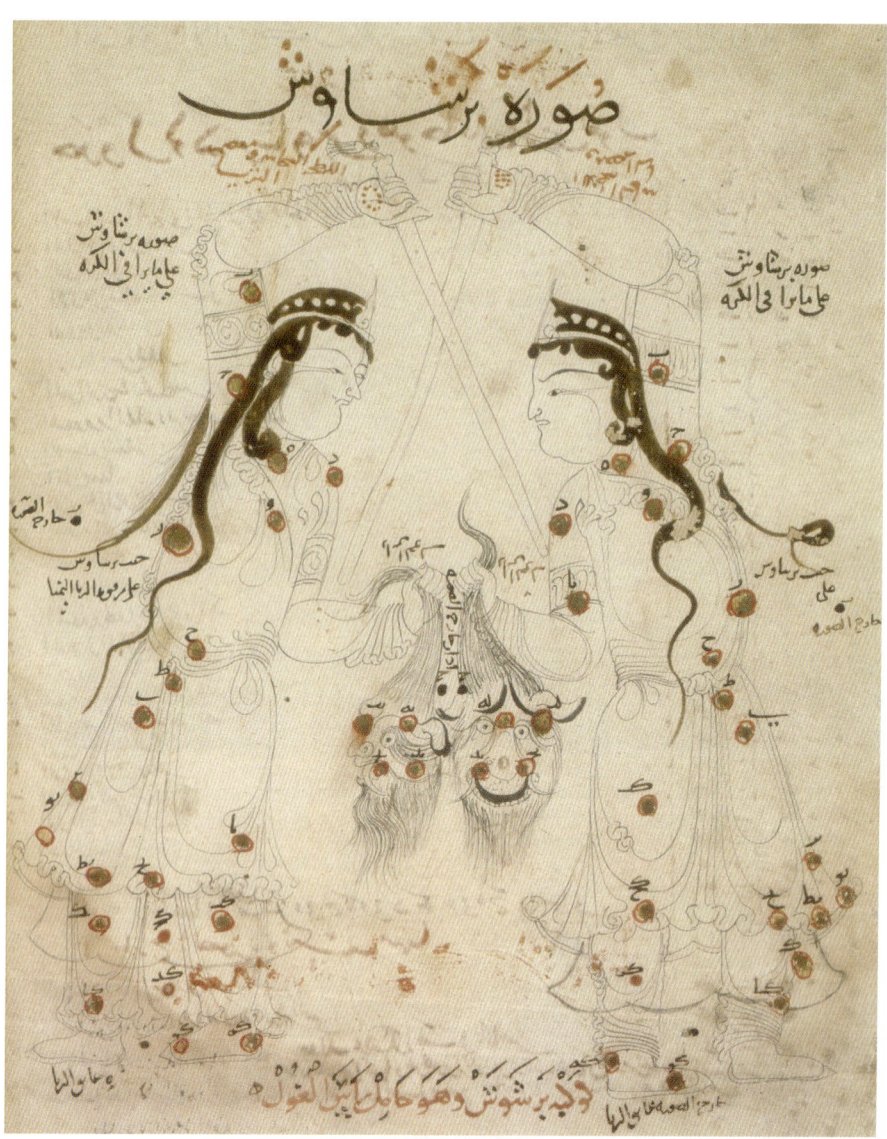

ABOVE: Perseus bearing the demon's head. A Persian representation of the constellation Perseus, who holds the head of Medusa, in accordance with the Greek legend in which Perseus kills the Gorgon Medusa, whose appearance is so terrible that any person that looks at her is turned to stone. The illustration is from the star catalogue of the tenth-century Persian astronomer Abd al-Rahman al-Sufi. The constellation is shown in double aspect, or reflected, in order to represent it as it would be seen from the earth and reversed, as on a star-globe.

ABOVE: The Grimace of Hell; a detail from Domenico di Pace Beccafumi's (1486–1551) *Christ in Limbo, c* 1530–5. Although not mentioned in the canonical gospels, Christ's Descent into hell is referred to in the Apostle's Creed ('He descended into Hell' before His Resurrection); it was also described in the apocryphal Gospel of Nicodemus, which was possibly written in the fifth century. Nicodemus recounts how Christ bursts open the gates of hell, binds Satan in chains, and leads all the 'patriarchs and prophets and martyrs and forefathers … out of Hell'. In this depiction, one of Satan's guardians of hell, a creature with claw-like hands, looks on helplessly with mouth agape in fear and awe as Christ appears to ravage his domain. Originally in the Church of San Francesco in Siena, Italy, the oil-on-wood painting is today in the Pinacoteca Nazionale, Siena, Italy.

RIGHT: Grotesques on the tomb of Prior Rowland Leschman at Hexham Abbey, Northumberland, England. The tomb dates from 1491, the year of Prior Leschman's death. A common Christian iconographic model from the ninth century to the Renaissance shows the Lord of Hell sitting on a throne, crushing a sinner under his feet; here, a cloven-footed demon (the horn of which is positioned where Satan's penis would be) peeps out, apparently unharmed, from between the legs of the seated figure. Clues that the latter represents Satan are the notched decorations on his head – they could either represent a crown or, more likely given the context, a flaming mane – and the figure's grim, merciless expression. Whether or not this reading is correct, the two grotesques peer outwards, acting as a reminder to the living that Satan will be ready to welcome sinners to hell on Judgement Day.

RIGHT: A demonic head with a vine banderol in its mouth; detail of a marble column in the Benedictine Abbey of Sacra di San Michele, Val di Susa, Italy. The column helps support the arch featuring the signs of the zodiac and other constellations that is situated at the top of the Abbey's Grand Staircase of the Dead, so-called because it is lined with tombs. The Abbey, which was founded in the tenth century and dissolved in 1622, was one of four sites in western Europe (with Michael's Mount in Cornwall, England, Mont Saint Michel in Normandy, France and the shrine of Monte Sant'Angelo on Mount Gargano in southern Italy) of particular importance because of their close association with the Archangel Michael. The zodiacal arch refers to Saint Michael's supremacy among the angels (as leader of the Celestial forces).

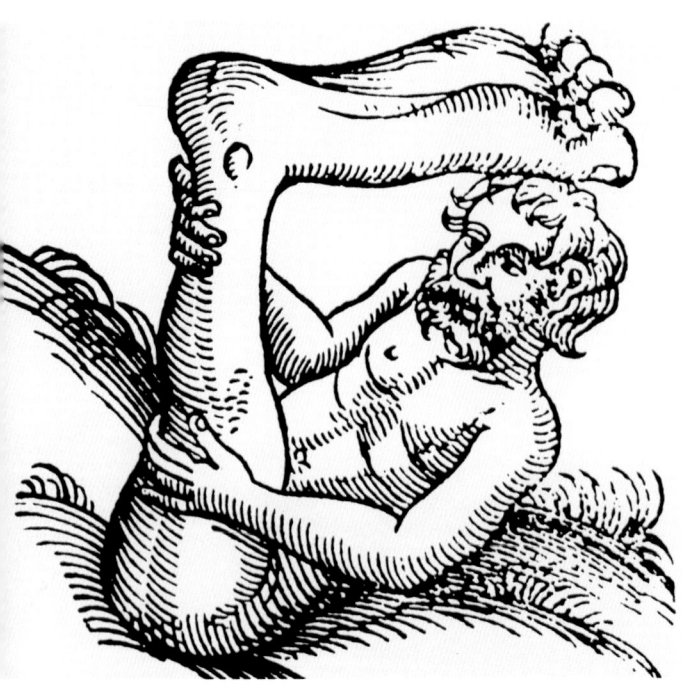

LEFT: A Sciopod, as depicted in Conrad Lycosthenes' (1518–61) *Prodigiorum ac ostentorum chronicon*, published in Basel, Switzerland in 1557. In her *Saracens, Demons and Jews*, Debra Higgs Strickland notes that although medieval thinkers drew a direct link between the physical deformity of the Monstrous Races and sinful behaviour, 'deformity was not always equated with sin'. Thus, although on one hand the one-legged Sciopod 'may be compared to the recluse who forgets his earlier vows through demonic trickery, so that by the storms of thought and the heat of temptation, he relies on his carelessness [his one large foot], with which he covers himself', 'the sheltering foot of the fast-moving [creature can also signify] the virtue of love, which allows people swift gains in the heavenly kingdom'.

OPPOSITE (BELOW): A Cynocephalus (dog-headed man), a Blemmyae, a Bicephalus, a Cyclope or Arimaspi, and a Sciopod; an illustration in Johann Herold's *Heydenwelt* of 1554. In the medieval imagination, as nature reflected God's will, external appearance reflected moral character: physical deformity was thus a sign of moral deformity. This, however, raised the question of why God had created the 'Monstrous Races' at all. Strickland comments that the most popular Christian explanation was that they were the descendants of Cain: 'Cain is the type for the unrepentant sinner … and Cain's progeny, having committed offences of their own, sired misshapen offspring'. Herold's work appeared towards the end of the late Middle Ages and, by the end of the sixteenth century, an evolution was underway in the way in which the Monstrous Races were perceived: increasingly, they were believed to be examples of fascinating natural wonders – as signs not of God's Wrath but of nature's fertility.

ABOVE: The Ewaipanoma or Blemmyae, shown in an illustration from part VI of the series of descriptions of foreign voyages published by Levinus Hulsius in Germany in 1599; this part describes Sir Francis Drake's 'famous voyage' – his circumnavigation of the world in 1577–80 in the *Golden Hind*. The long-held tradition that pagan 'Monstrous Races' inhabited remote parts of the world dated back to Classical civilization and was expanded in the Middle Ages, for example in the Anglo-Saxon *Marvels of the East* and *Liber monstrorum* (*Book of Monsters*). This illustration borrows from that tradition: the Blemmyae, with his face on his chest, was (along with the Epiphagus, who has eyes in his shoulders), the most often depicted of the Headless Men, or Acephali, in the medieval gallery of Monstrous Races. Given the significance of the head in mediaeval symbolism – as the seat of the intellect and soul, and as 'governor' of the body, the Blemmyae signified lack of intellect, self-control and spiritual awareness.

ABOVE: A gargoyle on the western facade of the thirteenth-century Cathedral of Our Lady of Amiens, Amiens, France. When seen from far below, it would appear that the gargoyle depicts a man fellating himself. Seen close-up as here the figure may in fact be eating a mandrake root. If this is correct, the stonemason was cleverly playing on the superstitions and legends surrounding the mandrake in his carving – for it was believed that the plant was endowed with mysterious powers. It could, for example, be used to expel demons from sick people, but it was also believed to be fatal to dig it up or even (under particular conditions) to touch it. Most important in this context, it was thought that excessive consumption of the plant's berries was said to cause madness and even death. Knowing what the gargoyle would seem to depict from below, and knowing what it actually portrayed, was the stonemason equating the madness of perverse sexual excess with the insanity that could result from touching and eating the mandrake?

ABOVE: A mantichora and other mythical beasts, together with angels; the Cathedral of Saint Etienne, Metz, France. The cathedral, which was built between 1220 and 1520, was constructed in part by joining two older buildings and then adding, in the fifteenth century, a transept and a choir. No expense was spared in building the great Gothic cathedrals, and money would have been lavished on elaborate stone-carvings such as these, even though the beautifully detailed work might not be clearly visible to the passers-by below. It was on these grounds that the great reviver (and transformer) of the Cistercian Order, Bernard of Clairvaux (c 1090–1153), had complained of the existence of similar grotesques in the Order's monasteries: 'What are these fantastic monsters doing in the cloisters under the very eyes of the brothers as they read? … Surely if we do not blush for such absurdities we should at least regret what we have spent on them.' Although Saint Bernard (he was canonized in 1174) became highly influential in twelfth-century church affairs, on the matter of grotesque stone-carvings his thoughts were clearly ignored – as the grotesques and gargoyles of the Gothic cathedrals attest.

Visions of Hell

The concept of a dark nether region in which those who have behaved badly in life will receive their 'just desserts' after death is, arguably, as old as humanity itself. The Ancient Greeks believed in an Underworld ruled by Hades (who, under the Romans, became Pluto), in which Sisyphus was doomed forever to push a boulder uphill, and Tantalus to attempt futilely to slake his thirst with water that runs away. For the Ancient Egyptians, the souls of the dead were weighed in the balance by the black, jackal-headed god Anubis. And in the Zoroastrianism of ancient Persia – near neighbours of the Hebrews – the souls of the dead had to pass over *cinvato pertush* (the 'accountant's bridge'), which stretched over the yawning abyss of hell, and into which evildoers were doomed to fall, while the good entered *garô demâna* (the life of bliss).

However, the notion of an afterlife of perpetual misery and punishment (or, for the virtuous, eternal bliss and reward) was most thoroughly developed, and reached its most elaborate visual expression, in Western Europe of the Middle Ages where, in the sculpted friezes of the portals of the great cathedrals and the painted altarpieces and wall paintings of churches and chapels, visions of hell loomed as starkly elaborate reminders of the importance of following the proper, Christian path in life. For those who went astray and turned their backs on God, the outcome was plain to see. And it did not make for comfortable viewing.

According to the Scriptures, hell was the final – and permanent – destination of those who had spurned God and refused to recognise Christ as their Saviour – and (important for the medieval church) it was where those who had committed all manner of sins on earth would be punished. The Scriptures furnished artists with sufficient clues as to the nature of hell. Matthew speaks of a 'furnace of fire' where 'there shall be weeping and gnashing of teeth' (13:42); Mark, of eternal torment with fire and worms; and Luke, of the heat and thirst suffered by the damned.

The artistic shorthand for hell was thus an abode of darkness with perpetual flames, worms, vermin and the like. In Last Judgement imagery – in which hell figured prominently – it was the opposite, in every way, of Paradise, the contorted suffering of the damned contrasting with the blessed calmness of the elect proceeding joyfully towards the gates of heaven. For the medieval viewer, one of the most terrifying aspects of such scenes would have been the demons populating them, and the dreadful alacrity with which they went about their infernal business.

This is not to say that the classical antecedents were forgotten. Indeed, nowhere was their influence more apparent than in Dante's *Divine Comedy* (written 1306–20), the first part of which (the Inferno) describes the Italian poet's downward journey, circle by circle, through the realm of lost souls in the company of the Latin poet Virgil, to the pit of hell at the dead – literally and spiritually – centre of the earth, where Satan sits, lumpen and frozen. In Dante's hell the punishments inflicted on sinners reflect their crimes in life – this was the concept of *contrapasso*, or counterpoint, whereby the punishment fits the crime. Dante's verses influenced medieval and Renaissance artists alike, as well as much later artists, including the nineteenth-century illustrator Gustave Doré.

ABOVE: This detail of the Damned from Michelangelo's Sistine Chapel fresco the *Last Judgement* (1536–41) depicts Charon, the ferryman from antiquity who conducts the dead across the river Styx, as a terrifying underworld figure true to Dante's description of him in his *Inferno* as a hoary demon beating those who lag behind with his oar. The damned are pushed and pulled off Charon's barque and driven into Hell by assistant demons with skins the colour of dead flesh; the expressions of terror on the faces of these souls consigned to Hell are more terrifying than any flames. Yet some, such as the figure half-covering his face in despair, offer no resistance, as though overcome with anguish in the realisation of the deeds that have brought them to this place of torment.

OPPOSITE (BELOW): A sculptural detail from a relief of hell, from the Last Judgement carved tympanum on the twelfth-century Cathedral of Saint-Lazare in Autun (Saône-et-Loire), France. *The Last Judgement* (*c* 1130–40), sculpted by Gislebertus, figures in the tympanum over the west (main) portal. This figure of a sorrowful sinner suffering the torments of hell appears on Christ's left, below the sculpted scene of souls being weighed. One of the most disturbing visions of hell in existence, this weak-looking condemned soul is literally in the inescapable and hugely powerful hands of the Devil. His open mouth conveys the aural discordance, as well as the physical and spiritual horrors of hell; for it is a place of horrid clamour, and filled with shrieking and wailing.

ABOVE: A relief on a Roman alabaster urn found at Volterra, in Italy, depicting the underworld figure of Charun, who in Roman art was always represented carrying a mallet. The ancient Romans believed that at the moment of death the soul was seized upon by two opposing groups of genii – those led by the malevolent Charun, and those summoned by Vanth, who was a benevolent spirit. The deceased were understood to travel to the underworld on foot, on horseback (as is shown here), or in a chariot. The Roman concept of the Infernal Regions borrowed heavily from that already mapped out in detail by the Greeks and the native Etruscans, but dwelt less on the poetic associations and the rich cast of characters of the latter – perhaps out of superstition, they were mindful not to elevate the gods of the underworld.

ABOVE: In this illustration by Gustave Doré for a nineteenth-century edition of *The Inferno* (1667), Dante and his guide, the Roman poet Virgil, observe sinners being tossed about by the waves in the watery abysses of the Infernal Regions. The concept of infernal rivers originated with the ancient Greeks, whose underworld comprised several subterranean watercourses: the Acheron (derived from the word for 'affliction'), with its affluent the Cocytus (fed by the Phlegethon), the Lethe and, finally, the Styx. According to Greek mythology, the Styx made nine loops around the underworld. Acheron was the river of sadness, while Cocytus was the river of lamentation, swollen with the tears of the dead.

OPPOSITE: 'Charon the ferryman' (*c* 1879) in an illustration by Gustave Doré for a nineteenth-century edition of John Milton's *Paradise Lost* (1667). In Greek mythology, Charon was the old man whose task it was to ferry the souls of the deceased across the Acheron, one of the rivers of the underworld, which in its lower reaches became the Styx. In order to be granted passage by the irascible old man, who was notoriously difficult to deal with, the 'shade' of the deceased newcomer had to present him with a coin (*obolus*), without which Charon would mercilessly drive away the ignorant intruder – from which legend the custom in classical times of putting a coin on the tongue of the deceased derived.

OPPOSITE: A naked woman is borne towards Hell by an enthusiastic horned and winged demon in this image, which is a detail from a fresco by Luca Signorelli depicting *The Torture of the Damned* in the Cappella Nuova in the cathedral in Orvieto, Italy. This crowded scene, which occupies a large area of one wall in the chapel, is populated by demons who are busily – and, as is shown here, often gleefully – performing their roles of tormenting the naked souls of sinners. The human dimensions and attributes of the demonic creatures, with their recognizable limbs, frames and even expressions, make the suffering they inflict on the sinners even more ghastly to behold. Here, the intertwined hands and fingers, and the clamping of human flesh against demonic flesh, translates in the viewer – as the artist fully intended – into a truly skin-crawling, physical revulsion.

ABOVE: *Fallen Angels entering Pandemonium, c* 1841, by the English artist John Martin (1789–1854). Martin was famous for his large apocalyptic landscapes. The visions expressed in them were, as in this fiery scene, so audacious that the artist received the nickname 'Mad Martin'. This densely detailed scene of tumult illustrates verses in Book I of John Milton's *Paradise Lost*. It was one of many scenes the artist made to illustrate Milton's epic poem. Indeed, a contemporary critic wrote, 'We know of no artist whose genius so perfectly fitted him to be the illustrator of the mighty Milton … and he has more than realized the highest of our hopes. There is a wildness, a grandeur and a mystery about his designs which are indescribably fine'. Martin's art exerted a powerful appeal on the Romantic imagination, especially in France where it became synonymous with the Sublime.

BELOW: The punishment in hell for the sin of Envy (Latin, *Invidia*) is depicted here as a miserable dousing in freezing water – *laqua freda*. The dark, bat-like demons use their pitchforks to propel the livid-red naked humans (fresh from a roasting in the flames of hell) into the cold water, relentlessly forcing them to submerge themselves.

Among the unfortunates are monks (who are recognizable by their tonsures), a king (with a crown) and a bishop (still wearing his mitre). This was not the only icy pool in hell, though; for in Dante's *Inferno* Satan is depicted as the cold heart of hell, whose infernal rivers are frozen by the icy gales which are created by the beating of his wings.

OPPOSITE (ABOVE): An illustration from a French illuminated manuscript (*c* 1450–70) depicting the punishments inflicted upon the lecherous in hell. Demons with tails, horns and talons toss the lechers, guilty as they are of the sin of Lust (Latin, *Luxuria*) – one of the Seven Deadly Sins – into a brick funnel, where, according to the iconography of the medieval Church, they are smothered in fire and brimstone. Lust was also associated with sloth, as the idle fell prey more readily to temptations of the flesh. In the fight against Lust the virtue of chastity, or temperance, had to be cultivated, reflecting the theory of psychomachy – the battle for the soul – which by the Middle Ages was a well-worn theme in Christian writing and art. It had its origins in the fifth-century epic poem *Psychomachia* by Prudentius, which charted the human struggle between vice and virtue.

OPPOSITE (BELOW): An illustration from a French illuminated manuscript (*c* 1450–70) depicting the punishments inflicted upon the slothful in hell. In medieval times, Sloth, or laziness (Latin, *Acedia*) was regarded as one of the Seven Deadly Sins, even if later it came to be viewed as mere physical idleness or a lack of creative inspiration. To the medieval Christian, *acedia* was most definitely a vice – a failure, through laziness, to love God with all of one's heart, mind and soul. Against this spiritual sloth was pitted the contrary virtue of diligence, with the religious zeal that this implied. Sloth was also associated with sadness, for mental and physical inactivity led to melancholy, and ultimately on to despair. In this image, the slothful are being eaten alive by carrion birds and dragons; a more common image of the time, however, was of the slothful being devoured by snakes.

LEFT: *The Barque of Dante* (1822) by Eugène Delacroix (1798–1863). This large canvas – Delacroix's first submission to the Salon, where it caused a sensation – shows Phlegyas, the infernal employee from Virgil's *Aeneid*, ferrying Dante and Virgil across the Styx to the infernal city of Dis. The fires of this city, which in Dante's *Inferno* encompassed all of hell from this point on, can be seen burning on the shore. Dante (left) is frightened by what he sees, but Virgil is inured to the horrors of hell. Here, in its fifth circle – in the swampy waters of the Styx – the sin of anger is punished; the wrathful, expressing their anger, attack one another (bottom right), while the sullen, repressing their rage, stew beneath the surface of the muddy swamp. All are confined to the Styx, although some try to escape their fate by hanging onto the barque.

ABOVE: An illuminated page from a Book of Hours made in France *c* 1407; its creator is known only as the Master of the Brussels Initials. This intricately made illustration, with a decorated border comprised of figures, foliage and birds, is taken from the Penitential Psalms and Litany. The scene shows the damned being driven into hell, the entrance to which is a gaping, burning hole in the upper part of the illustration, where the familiar earthly sights of towns, turrets and battlements are also depicted. The damned – whose ranks include monks, pilgrims, women, kings and a bishop – are goaded by hairy devils and bat-like devils with wings; these demons push them in carts, carry them in baskets and pull them on ropes, down into hell itself – here depicted as a turreted structure in the lower half of the illustration. In hell, the terrified sinners are shown to be disembowelled, roasted and basted over fires or cooked in a cauldron, while at the centre of this scene of eternal misery, Satan himself devours the naked souls of the damned. Throughout the scene snakes slither and chew at the flesh of the unfortunate sinners.

LEFT: A page from the *Bedford Book of Hours*, an illuminated manuscript produced for the wedding of John, Duke of Bedford, to Anne of Burgundy in 1423. The scene depicts the Last Judgement, with the resurrected Christ sitting in judgement on the world and, as the gospel of Saint Matthew describes it (Matt. 25:33), separating sheep from goats as a shepherd does with his flock. In this representation, the righteous rise up from their graves to be crowned by angels on their way to the kingdom of God, while the damned are dragged into Hell – the mouth of the monster Leviathan – by demons. The mouth of Hell corresponds to the description of Leviathan in the book of Job: 'Out of his mouth go burning lamps, and sparks of fire leap out.' (Job 41:19). On Christmas Eve 1430, seven years after her wedding, Anne – with the consent of her husband – presented the *Bedford Hours* as a gift to their nephew King Henry VI, prior to his coronation.

OPPOSITE: Detail from the central panel of *The Last Judgement* triptych, *c* 1500, by Hieronymus Bosch, which may be seen in the Akademie der Bildenden Künste, Vienna, Austria. Unusually, the torments of hell loom large in this central panel; seeping, as it were, from the right-hand panel of hell itself. Depicted here in the middle panel, though, is a veritable hell on Earth. Christ sits in judgement, but there is no sign of the risen dead (the sentence having been passed some time before, perhaps?). The picture is dominated by images of cutting, slicing, stabbing and piercing, possibly in reference to the dual sins of gluttony and anger. Human figures are put on spits and roasted, or they are broiled – or indeed, as here, pan-fried, to accompany two eggs. The complacent yet diabolical chef with the feet of a chicken gazes up at more skewered humans, which are ready for a roasting.

ABOVE: Jan Brueghel the Elder, *Orpheus in the Underworld*, 1594. Orpheus, recognizable by his harp, is portrayed in the underworld into which, according to Greek myth, he had descended to rescue his wife, the nymph Eurydice. Jan Brueghel's vision of the infernal regions of the afterlife was an amalgam of medieval Christian concepts of hell, and pagan, classical visions of the underworld; such mixing of Christian belief with imagery and characters from Greek myth was typical of the Renaissance, and was due mainly to the description found in Dante's *Inferno*, which used Virgil's *Aeneid* as a source for the geography of hell. Hell is shown here as populated by demonic insects and freakish, reptilian creatures, along with the naked human souls whom they torment; the fires of the city of Dis burn in the background, illuminating a ghastly torture wheel. Presiding over this dark kingdom are Hades and Persephone, rulers of the underworld, whom Orpheus must charm with his lyre to secure the release of Eurydice.

ABOVE: A scene from the series of illustrations depicting Infernal Punishments for the Seven Deadly Sins which appeared in *Le Grant Kalendrier et Compost des Bergiers* by Nicolas Le Rouge, 1523. This repellent scene shows the punishments meted out to those guilty of the sin of Gluttony (Latin, *Gula*, from the word 'throat') in hell. The gluttons are force-fed disgusting food and drink by brightly coloured devils, more of whom continue to arrive to replenish the jars and plates which are laden with toads. One devil even 'feeds' the sinner in the centre with his own tongue. Along with Lust, Gluttony was one of the sins of the flesh (*vitia carnalia*), generally thought of as less heinous than the five other 'deadly sins'. The link between Gluttony and Lust was based on the biblical temptation by Eve of Adam with the apple, and also with her physical charms. Elsewhere, gluttons are often depicted as constrained by demons from eating from a sumptuously laid table spread before them.

ABOVE: A scene from the series of illustrations depicting Infernal Punishments for the Seven Deadly Sins which appeared in *Le Grant Kalendrier et Compost des Bergiers* by Nicolas Le Rouge, 1523; it was an almanac that served also an a moral manual, aimed at teaching the 'science of the shepherds' (*les bergers*) to lay people. This illustration depicts the fate of the slothful in the next world – consigned to Hell for this Deadly sin of spiritual Lethargy, they are thrown into pits where they are devoured by snakes. Although the sin of Sloth is here shown as receiving its just deserts in hell, it became much less frequently depicted as a vice with the waning of the Middle Ages, to become a rare motif in Renaissance depictions of Virtues and Vices. For the medieval viewer of this image, though, it would have reminded him or her or the certainty of judgement in the next life.

LEFT: An 1862 illustration by Gustave Doré for Dante's *Divine Comedy* (*c* 1321), showing Dante and his guide Virgil after they have arrived in the city of Dis in the sixth circle of hell (canto 9). They are now in the lower regions of hell, where the more serious – and active – sins are punished. To reach Dis, Dante and Virgil have had to cross the swampy Styx; because the city's iron walls were guarded by fallen angels in the shape of monstrous demons, it was only by the intervention of an angel from heaven that they were able to penetrate them. Inside, they are met by a mournful vista – a plain scattered with sarcophagi licked by flames, from which escape lamentable moans. It is here, in the sixth circle, that the arch-heretics – those who failed to believe in God and the afterlife – are punished.

OPPOSITE: An illustration by Gustave Doré for a nineteenth-century edition of Dante's *Divine Comedy*, showing Dante and Virgil in the third chasm, or bolgia, of the *malebolge* – the eighth circle of hell. Dante, peering forward, observes more closely those guilty of simony (canto 19); these were those guilty of abusing their power within the Church. Among the simonists are popes and Dante mistakenly takes one of them to be Pope Boniface, whereas this papal sinner was in fact Pope Nicholas III in life. The confusion is altogether natural because of the nature of the punishment – to be wedged head down into a stone hole. The *contrapasso* is particularly apt, for these holes are fiery 'baptismal fonts', into which the sinners have been stuffed upside down so that, instead of the baptismal water moistening their heads, the flames of damnation are licking their feet – possibly fed by the 'fat' they claimed for their own in life.

LEFT: An illustration by Gustave Doré for a nineteenth-century edition of Dante's *Divine Comedy*, showing Dante and his guide Virgil in the sixth circle of hell (canto 10). Doleful moans and sighs are audible from the brazier-like sarcophagi, and from one of the tombs rises up the historical figure of Farinata degli Uberti (*d* 1264), who led the Ghibelline faction in Florence. He and Dante are natural enemies, for the Ghibellines defeated the Guelphs, Dante's party, in 1248 and 1260; both times the Guelphs returned to power a few years later. The pair exchange frosty words, which conclude with Farinata explaining that the 'shades' (the deceased) can predict events in the future, but are unable to make any sense of the present.

ABOVE: A detail from a depiction of hell (*c* 1500–10) produced by the workshop of the artist Hieronymus Bosch, *c* 1450–1516. The painting is in the Hermitage museum in Saint Petersburg, Russia. Hell is here a truly incandescent city, in keeping with Dante's description of the infernal city of Dis as encircled by iron walls from which rise red towers that are continually ablaze. Although the fires of hell burn eternally, the city is never destroyed. Here, legions of tiny, naked human souls are being pursued and tortured by demons which have hideous animal and insect forms, none of which, however, is as hideous as the giant, quasi-human face whose missing lower half forms the gaping mouth of Hell. There is no evidence here of Dante's self-contained circles of hell, with their sophisticated gradations of sin; here, instead, is a horrific, melting-pot of suffering. Its horror is in its very chaos, unfurling against the rust-coloured backdrop of sulphurous ever-burning flames.

ABOVE: Arguably one of the most famous depictions of hell, this musical inferno unfolding before a scene of fire and ice constitutes the right-hand panel of the triptych *The Garden of Earthly Delights* (c 1500) by Hieronymus Bosch, now in the Prado Museum, Madrid, Spain. Although devils in the traditional sense are absent, all those present in the scene (except for the enigmatic, decapitated 'tree man' in the centre) are undergoing some form of suffering. A monstrous chariot made up of two giant ears flanking a huge knife rolls forward, crushing figures indiscriminately beneath it; wild beasts, armour-plated insects and reptiles – composite creatures created in Bosch's prodigious imagination out of parts of real or mythical creatures – prod, pierce and goad their victims. The significance of the melancholy white face (which is perhaps a self-portrait of the artist) shown beneath a mill-wheel hat, and with dead tree trunks for legs and an excavated egg for a body, remains a mystery.

ABOVE: *The Infernal Gridiron*, a miniature painting from the *Très Riches Heures du Duc de Berry*, which was made before 1416. Produced by the Limbourg brothers, this illuminated manuscript was one of the most lavish visual documents created during the Middle Ages. Satan, wearing a crown – as Lord of the Infernal Realm – is depicted reclining on a gridiron, whose red-hot embers are kept continually burning by air which is forced from the huge bellows on either side, and worked by two demons with the aid of a complex system of ropes and pulleys. These demons and the other devils combine goat and human traits, and all sport bats' wings and horns. Satan devours the souls of the damned, which are also wedged into the gridiron, there to burn for all eternity.

RIGHT: An engraving, finished in watercolour, by Carlo Lasinio, of the fresco of hell painted *c* 1330–40 on the walls of the Campo Santo, the monumental cemetery of Pisa. Its creator was the Tuscan painter Buonamico Buffalmacco. The frescos – of which this was only one scene (the others included a Triumph of Death and a Last Judgement) – were badly damaged in the bombing Pisa suffered during World War II. Their imagery would have reminded the fourteenth-century Pisans who came to the Campo Santo cemetery – one of the city's most public spaces – of the sermons of the local Dominican preachers. Satan is armour-plated and in each of his three mouths he crunches a sinner, while others are gripped in his clawed hands. Those he has consumed are seen in fiery torments inside his body, before they are excreted into Hell's eternal fires. Hell is depicted as a multi-chambered infernal place, reflecting Dante's divisions of hell into circles throughout which every kind of sin, and sinner, is catered for.

ABOVE: Devil stuffing the dragon into hell, from the *Tanner Apocalypse*, an English Apocalypse manuscript from the third quarter of the thirteenth century, now in the Bodleian Library, Oxford. The entrance to hell is here depicted as a large, feline hell-mouth. Such 'Apocalypse' manuscripts were common in the Middle Ages, and referred to the final part of the New Testament, the Book of Revelation of Saint John the Divine, also known as Saint John of Patmos. The final part of Revelation describes the defeat of Satan, who here appears in the form of the dragon being tossed into hell. The green devil has a prominent and expressive face on its belly, from its mouth spews a flame situated precisely where a penis should be – a sign of much-despised demonic carnality.

ABOVE: This image of Satan devouring souls in hell is a detail from the Last Judgement frescos by Giorgio Vasari and Federico Zuccari, which decorate the interior of the cupola of the Duomo (the Cathedral of Santa Maria del Fiore) in Florence, Italy. Vasari (*b* 1511) was the artist behind the scheme, and executed a third of it before his death in 1574, after which his friend Zuccari (1540–1609) completed the decoration. Zuccari's was a startling rendering of hell, his powerful devils having been influenced by Luca Signorelli's frescos in the cathedral of Orvieto. The unrepentant bodies of the damned are tossed into the furnace, from which red flames and bloody embers illuminate the infernal regions with a rust-coloured glow. The bodies of two flayed, semi-dissected sinners perch either side of the abyss, one praying – too late – for salvation, the other zombie-like and mute. Satan, in the form of a goat with monstrous bestial wings, rears up from the pit chewing on a naked sinner.

OPPOSITE: A detail of hell, from Fra Angelico's *Last Judgement* (*c* 1431) altarpiece, now in the Museo di San Marco, Florence, Italy. The artist's vision of hell shows the influence of Dante's *Divine Comedy*, with its nine descending circles of hell – here depicted as chambers – and each circle representing a different sin, and with its own punishment. Yet while borrowing from the poet, Fra Angelico did not follow Dante's descending order of increasing sinful awfulness. The gluttonous (in the third circle in Dante's *Inferno*) sit round a table midway down, unable to eat the food spread out before them (a punishment meted out to the Greek mythological figure of Tantalus, who was eternally tortured by hunger and thirst for having stolen the ambrosia and nectar of the gods on Olympus), while a miser (in Dante, consigned to the fourth circle) is having molten gold poured down his throat close to the pit of hell, where Satan – a dark-skinned, horned monster – sits in a simmering pool.

m edib'eue . et firene m delubris uoluptatis . Jte ysaias xxxiiij .
Et erit cubile demonu̅ et pastua struciouis et occurret demoia.
honocentauruus et pilosus clamabunt alter ad alterum .

ABOVE: Illustration from the *Livre de la Vigne de Nostre Seigneur, c* 1450–70. The manuscript, which is now in the Bodleian Library, Oxford, was an illustrated treatise on the Antichrist, the Last Judgement, Heaven and Hell. On this page, the damned – here, all of them are male – are shown inside the gaping jaws of hell, where they are being tormented by an astonishing array of demons. The work's remarkable collection of demons fuelled its fame, and it was this aspect that most appealed to Francis

Douce, the late eighteenth-century collector who acquired the elaborately illuminated manuscript. Most horrible among these demons is the centaur-like creature at the centre who is wielding a flesh-hook and whose cloven feet trample two naked sinners. All of the infernal creatures, with the exception of the basilisks (creatures which were half-dragon and half-snake), have muzzles – their animal mouths twisted into grimaces – as well as pointed ears and horns like those of an ibex.

የጸድቃን።እኩ።ርኅብኩ።ወአብላዕነ።ነው።ነ
ተይከሙ።ወዓረቁ።ወ አበስከሙ።ነይ ይ ደ ይ ኩ።
ፈነግ ደ ።ኮን ኩ።ወ ተ ወ ክ ፍ ክ ሙ።ነተ ፋ ምቃ ለ ኩ።
ኅ ቤ የ ።ወን ነ በ ብ ክ ሙ ።ነ ይ ወ ይ ቤ ።እ ግ ዚ ኤ ።ማ አ ዜ
ጸጋ የ ።ወ ማ ፃ ጋ ።ግ ል ፃ ም ።ወ ይ ቤ ።ስ ሙ ።ር ።አ ሙ ።ር
ብ ለ ዕ ክ ሙ ።ነ ጸ ዳ ሩ ን ።ኩ ።ወ ኄ ። ይ ከ ተ ይ ።ክ ሙ ።ነ ነ ና
ገ ከ ከ ሙ ።ነ ደ ይ ።ኩ ።ወ እ ሐ ወ ጽ ክ ሙ ።ነ ኅ ነ ግ ።ይ
ክ ፍ ክ ሙ ።ነ ተ ተ ም ቃ ሕ ሕ ።ወ እ ም ጻ ጸ ።ክ ሙ ።ኅ ቤ
ሙ ።ነ ወ ይ ቤ ።ሱ ።ጎ ጥ ኤ ።ኅ ግ እ ዚ ኤ ።ኅ ቤ ።ር ።ር ።
ወ ኢ የ ሳ ላ ዕ ና ።ክ ዘ ።ው ።ጽ ም ።እ ክ ።ወ ኢ የ ል ተ ይ ና
ያ ል ብ ስ ና ።ክ ።ጽ ።ወ ።የ ከ ።ወ ።እ ሐ ወ ጽ ።ር ።ኮ ።ነ ገ ግ
ወ ክ ፍ ና ።ነ ።ሙ ።ቀ ሐ ።ር ።ነ ።ወ ።እ ።ጻ ።እ ።ነ ።ኅ ቤ ።ኩ
።ወ ይ ።ቤ ።ሙ ።እ ግ ።ዚ ።ኤ ።ዘ ።ዘ
ሐ ዱ ።እ ።ም ።እ ።ን ።አ ።ጎ ።ነ ።ነ ።ስ ።ተ
።ሐ ።ፋ ።እ ።ም ።ፍ ።ደ ።ር ።ማ ።ክ ።
።ዘ ።ለ ።ል ።ጻ ።ም ።ዘ ።ር ።ለ ።ል ።ው ።ለ ።ስ
።ማ ።ስ ።ክ ።ቲ ።ው ።

ዘ ክ ም ።ይ ።ስ ።ሕ ።ብ ።ም ።ሙ ።እ ።ግ ።ን ።ት ።ስ ።ነ ።ፋ ።ላ ።ት ።ጎ ።ጥ ።እ ።
በ ።ስ ።ና ።ስ ።እ ።ኅ ።ት ።ክ ።ም ።ይ ።ደ ።ይ ።ም ።ው ።ው ።ክ ።ተ ።ገ ።ገ ።ነ ።ም

እ ።ሱ ።እ ።ም ።ን ።ቱ ።እ ።ግ ።ን ።ት ።እ

ሲ ።አ ።ሕ ።ማ
ኅ ።ደ ።ረ ።አ ።ገ
።ት ።

ABOVE: A clutch of cheerful-looking devils with their trawl of sinners, whom they have bound in chains and are now gleefully torturing with burning flames. They appear to be in consultation with one another; exchanging views, perhaps, on how best to administer their torments. This illustration is from an Ethiopic manuscript entitled *The Miracles of the Blessed Virgin Mary*, made c 1632–67; the scene depicted is from the section that details the second coming of Christ and the Last Judgement. It graphically illustrates the eternal suffering – the 'everlasting punishment' (Matthew 25:46) – that lies in store in the next world for those who have not lived righteously in this one; the damned will be thrown 'into everlasting fire, prepared for the devil and his angels.' (Matthew 25:41).

ABOVE: The classical rulers of the ancient Greek underworld, Pluto and Persephone, survey their infernal domain in this painting from the first half of the seventeenth century. At first glance the tiny figures, picked out in yellow and gold, have the appearance of acrobats or entertainers, the whole almost passing for an elaborate, wheeling circus. However, the huge altar-like monument on the left is littered with skeletons (animal and human) and piled with human skulls. Diminutive demons with mask-like faces goad and torture the damned, and break them on the wheel visible in the distance. The overriding effect is of a place of Stygian gloom – to quote the Larousse *Encyclopedia of Mythology*, describing the primitive underworld of the ancient Greeks, 'a sort of dismal house of retirement [where] only the outstandingly guilty suffered eternal torture'.

OPPOSITE (ABOVE): An 1862 illustration by Gustave Doré for Dante's *Divine Comedy* (c 1321), showing the demon Malacoda tormenting the barrators, or grafters (those who acquired money by fraudulent means in their lives), in cantos 21–22 of the *Inferno*. This was just one scene from the multi-gulfed eighth circle of hell, which was very close to the earth's core and thus nearing Satan himself. It was in this circle, called the *malebolge* (the 'bad circle'), that the multifarious sins of fraudulence were punished. The eighth circle was in turn comprised of ten sub-circles, or *bolgias*. The barrators are punished in the fifth bolgia, or chasm, by being doomed to swim submerged in boiling pitch; if they should surface for more than a few seconds, their flesh is torn by the claws of the demons. Here, an escaping sinner is plunged back into the boiling pitch by Malacoda.

OPPOSITE (BELOW): An engraving showing the monstrous three-headed dog Cerberus, who guarded the entrance to Hades, the Greek underworld in classical times. In his epic poem the *Aeneid*, the Roman poet Virgil describes Cerberus as loud, huge and terrifying; his voice of bronze deafening the damned. Sometimes Cerberus is depicted with up to 50 serpents' heads (here his tail is a serpent) and drooling black venom. To get past him, the Sybil (who is Aeneas' guide) feeds the monstrous hound with a honey-cake, which makes him fall fast asleep. In Dante's *Inferno* too, Cerberus – along with several other pagan demons – guards the gates of Hell. In Greek mythology, Hercules on one occasion vanquished Cerberus, carrying him up to earth where the beast infected certain herbs with his venom, which were thereafter used in magic potions.

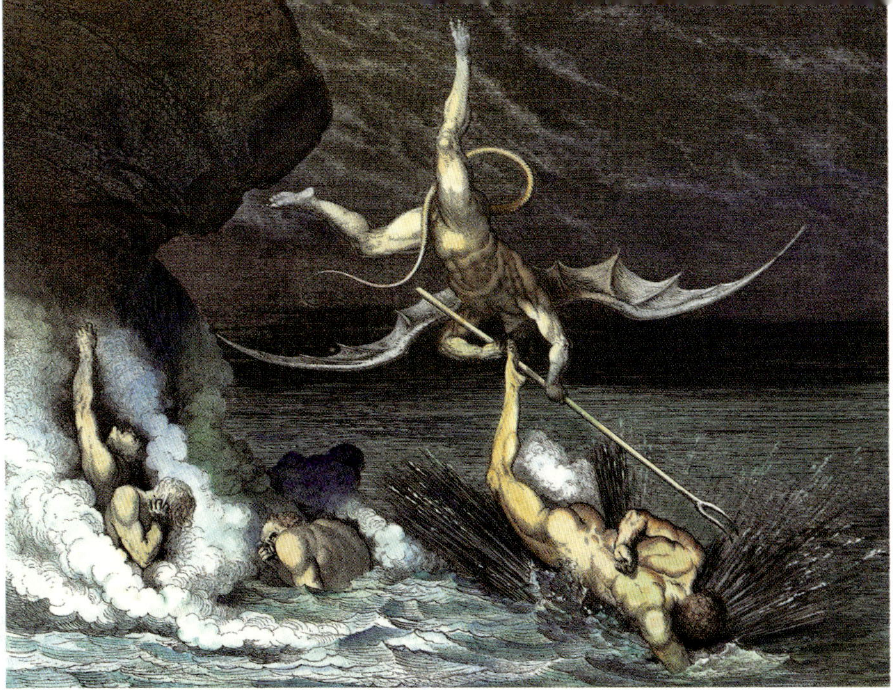

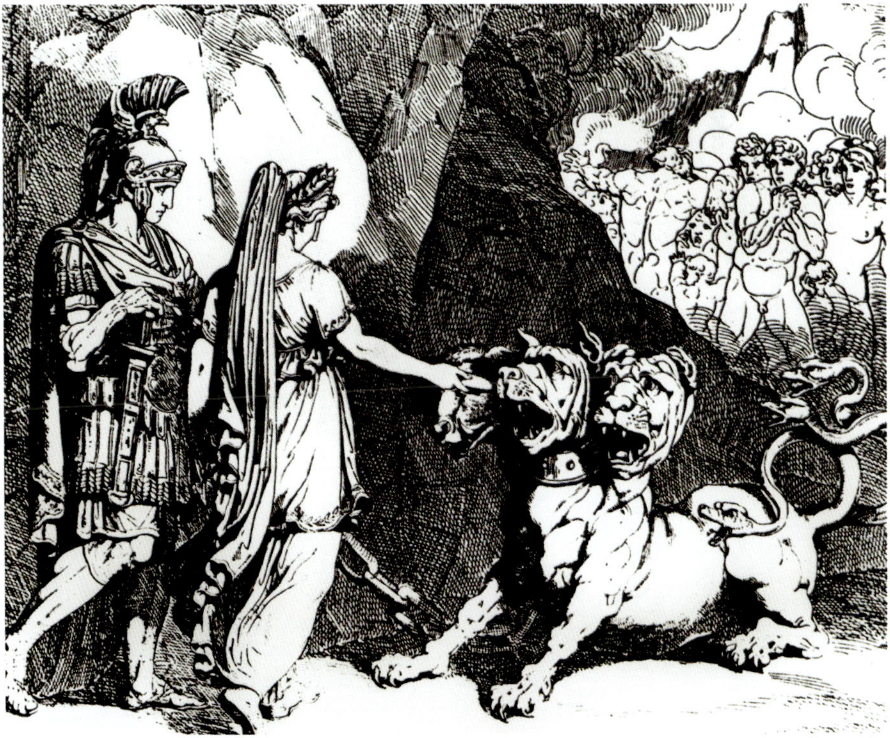

OPPOSITE: This illustration of Lucifer in a hell licked by tongues of fire is after a colourful original from the late twelfth-century *Hortus Deliciarum* (*Garden of Delights*), which is now lost. This was an elaborate illuminated manuscript – probably the work of several artists – made between 1176 and 1196 under the aegis of Herrad of Landsberg, abbess of the Saint Odile nunnery at Hohenbourg in Alsace. It treated the history of the world from the beginning to the end of time. Here, within a dark, four-tiered demonic complex, the damned are tortured. Christian belief of the time was that Jews were damned for being both 'enemies of the Faith' and responsible for the murder of Christ. Thus in the third tier on the left, a demon plunges a Jew – naked except for his funnel cap – into a purpose-built cauldron labelled *Judaei*, which already contains several other Jews visible as heads wearing hats. To the right, a cauldron labelled *armati milites* is earmarked for Christian knights; thus enemies from both within and outside the Church are targeted. Below, a monk holding a money bag is led by a demon. On Satan's lap sits a small, nude Antichrist; Satan's throne is alive – the animal heads of its arms devour tiny souls, and taloned feet crush the heads of the damned.

ABOVE: A detail from a mosaic depicting hell, from the Last Judgement in the cupola (ceiling vault) of the Baptistery in Florence, Italy. The latter's elaborate mosaic confection, inspired by the Byzantine mosaics of Ravenna and Venice, dates from the thirteenth and early fourteenth centuries. The pattern of the mosaics is arranged into six concentric tiers, centering on the lantern, with the judging Christ occupying almost an entire segment of the octagonal vault. This section was executed by Coppo di Marcovaldo between 1260 and 1276. Its terrifying representation of hell (at Christ's left hand) shows devils stuffing the damned into hell, which is dominated by the gigantic figure of Satan, bearded and with horns, and where they are consumed not just by the Prince of Evil, but also by hideous beasts, including toads and snakes. The Florentine Dante Alighieri would have known these mosaics, and was no doubt inspired by the grisly depiction of hell.

LEFT: Detail of the fresco *The Torture of the Damned* (*c* 1499–1504) by Luca Signorelli. The fresco, which is still *in situ* in the Cappella Nuova in the cathedral in Orvieto, Italy, was one of a cycle of frescos in the chapel depicting 'End Time' imagery. Included were scenes from the Reign of the Antichrist, the Last Judgement, the Resurrection of the Dead, the heavenly rewards of the blessed, and the torture of the damned in hell. All were depicted with startling Renaissance clarity. Here, the figures of both the sinners and their tormentors are life-size, and the tangle of anatomically observed human torsos and limbs – for, unusually, the bodies of the demons have recognizable human frames and muscles, albeit of a ghastly colouring and crowned by horns – makes for a particularly realistic and painful spectacle of human suffering. The demons tear at the flesh of the damned, whose classically rendered human forms grant a tragic quality to their torments.

ABOVE: A depiction of hellish carnage dating from *c* 1730–5 and painted on vellum, from an Ethiopic manuscript of the Revelation of Saint John. It shows decapitations in progress, with the hacked-off heads of humans and animals alike (goats, horses, lions, even slaughtered birds) strewn about the scene, and a lake of blood forming in the foreground. The illustration elaborates on a scene from the Book of Revelation, the last book of the New Testament, in which a verse (20:4) refers to the souls of those 'that were beheaded for the witness of Jesus, and for the word of God, and which had not worshipped the beast, neither his image.' Those depicted here are thus Christian martyrs, being slain by pained-looked angels; in Revelation the martyrs are described as alive with Christ for his 1,000-year reign, before the end of time and the final defeat of Satan.

OPPOSITE: An illustration depicting the damned writhing in the flames of hell, from a French illuminated manuscript of the Middle Ages. The concept of hell as an utterly dark place with perpetual flames was a prospect that was very real in the mind of the medieval Christian. Indeed, the 'hell fire' was the most conspicuous feature of the descriptions of the infernal place referred to in the Gospels of Matthew, Mark and Luke. For artist and illuminator, its flames evoked, in convenient shorthand, the punishment that lay in store for the unrepentant sinner. Bolstered by apocryphal texts, the image of punishment in the next life by eternal fire also armed preachers with stirring material with which to urge their congregations to keep on the straight and narrow path.

OPPOSITE: *The Simoniac Pope*, an illustration in pen and ink and watercolour on paper, by William Blake for a nineteenth-century edition of Dante's *Divine Comedy*. Here, Blake envisions canto 19 of the *Inferno*, in which Dante describes the consequences of the sin of simony – that is, the abuse of power by men of the Church while they were alive. Dante did not spare the popes, God's vicars on earth, from the torments of hell; indeed he places the corrupt popes in a very deep circle, the *malebolge*, which was the eighth of the nine circles of the Inferno. Blake shows the simoniac pope Nicholas III being vigorously tossed into the stone hole that will be his infernal abode. Blake's depiction of Dante's verses conveys a boiling energy, from the pitched-forward pose of the tormentor, who is already poised with another soul to be tossed head-first into the flames, to the billowing clouds of smoke and the flames burning the soles of the pope's feet.

ABOVE: An illustration by Gustave Doré for a nineteenth-century edition of Dante's *Divine Comedy* (c 1321), depicting the underworld judge Minos in the second circle of hell (canto five). Dante's Minos was an amalgam of two figures from classical mythology: Minos, the son of Zeus and Europa (who won the office of 'supreme judge of the underworld' because of his wisdom), and the fabled Cretan ruler King Minos, who kept the minotaur. The terrible coils wrapped around Minos as depicted here, however, were entirely of Dante's own imagining. Minos uses this long tail to assign the appropriate circle of hell to each sinner presented to him, by wrapping it around his body – the number of coils indicating to which layer of hell the sinner should be consigned.

LEFT: Fra Angelico painted a number of altarpieces on the theme of the Last Judgement; in this triptych, now displayed in Berlin, hell occupies the narrow, right-hand panel, as seen here. In its dreadful chambers, dark- and livid-skinned demons wield iron hooks and spears and inflict their tortures on the damned. At top right, beneath the entrance to hell (a funnel) they force those guilty of gluttony to eat snakes and swallow disgusting liquids; below the gluttonous the envious are consigned to a cauldron; below them, the libidinous are punished. At bottom left, the miserly are force-fed molten gold, while above them, the wrathful tear at their own flesh and strike one another; above them, the slothful writhe in a pit of snakes.

OPPOSITE (ABOVE): An illustration by Sandro Botticelli made to illuminate canto 15 of Dante's *Inferno*. Created in the early Renaissance (c 1494), this edition, with over 90 images by the artist, is known as the Medici Codex of the *Divine Comedy*; it is now in the Vatican Library, Rome. Botticelli's vision chimes with Dante's written description. In the seventh circle of hell, the sins of violence are punished; this circle comprises a plain of sand on which fire continually rains down. In canto 15, Dante and Virgil walk along a stone bank by a dyke; the sin they observe is sodomy, punishable by having to lie for a century in a rain of fire, whose red flecks are here seen spattered over the naked souls of the damned. Sodomy was regarded as a violent offence against God, and Dante draws on the biblical destruction of Sodom with fire and brimstone. The tiny figures here resemble minute acrobats, their wheeling limbs expressing the convulsions of the damned.

OPPOSITE (BELOW): *Dante, Allegory of the Divine Comedy and city of Florence*, by Domenico di Michelino, c 1465. In the foreground stands Dante, holding his famous work *La Divina Commedia* (The Divine Comedy), 1306–21. On the right is Florence, with its famous dome (not built in Dante's life); on the left, a vision of hell. The souls of the damned are marched by demons in a half-circle down into the funnel of Hell, with its nine, downward-spiralling circles. In the background rises the mount of purgatory, which, according to Dante's vision, consisted of seven terraces, corresponding to the Seven Deadly Sins, on the summit of which was Paradise. Purgatory was the place where penitents who awaited the final journey to paradise continually reaffirmed their faith and atoned for the sins they had committed on earth. For his journey through Purgatory in quest of spiritual purification and paradise, Dante exchanges his guide Virgil for Beatrice.

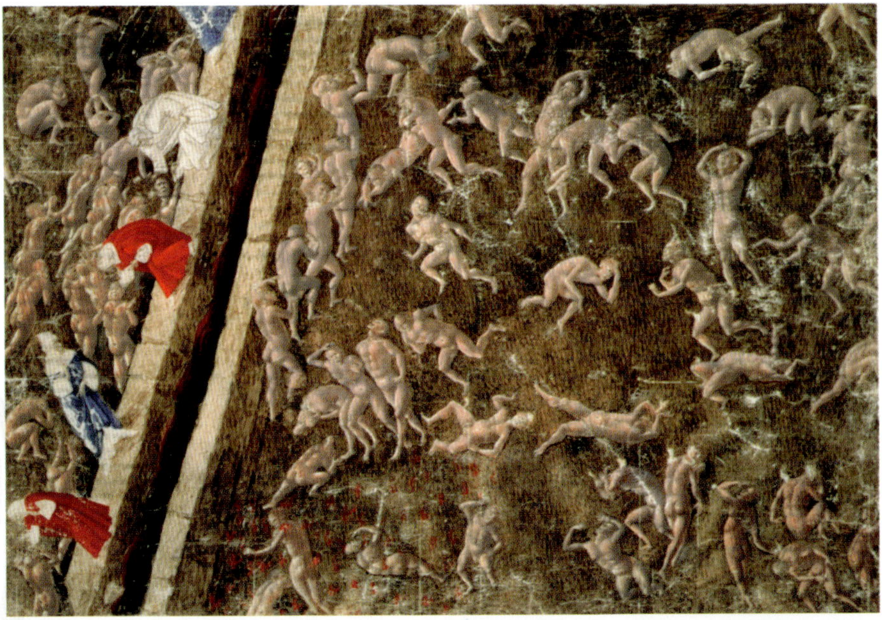

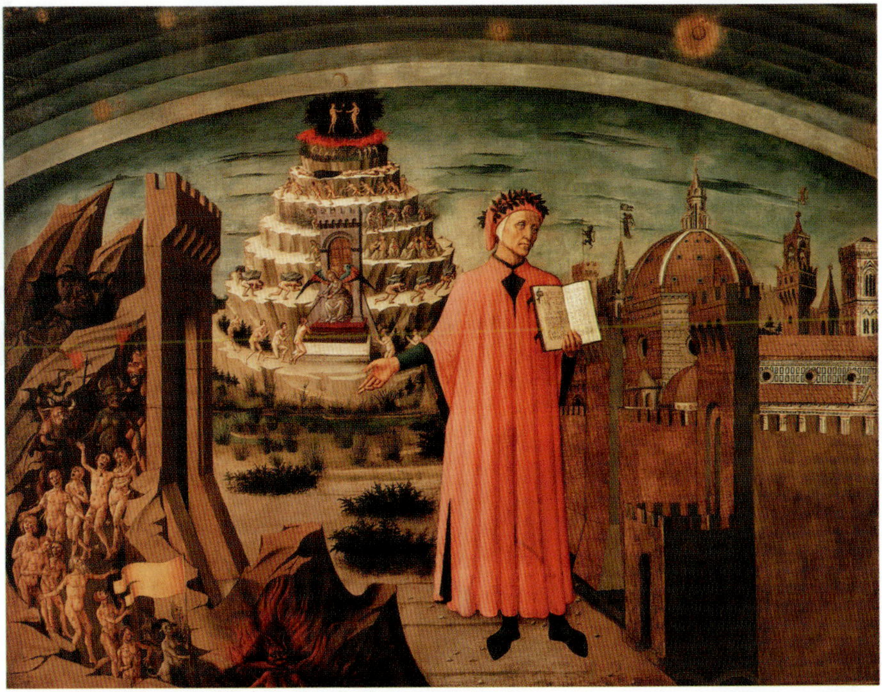

OPPOSITE: A painted panel depicting the damned falling towards hell, from the right-hand side of the *Last Judgement* altarpiece. The triptych, made for the church of Saint Mary in Gdansk, Poland was painted by the Northern Renaissance artist Hans Memling. With acute realism, the artist depicted the lost souls physically plunging into hell, not sparing the viewer their palpable terror at the first sight of its dreadful, eternal fires. The damned recoil, but to no avail – their fate has been determined, and their descent into hell is hastened by dark-skinned devils. A dreadful devil, with long, thin limbs and eyes glowing like white-hot coals, hooks a sinner to speed his fall, while clamping the neck of another poor soul with one of his taloned feet.

ABOVE: Detail of a Last Judgment scene from a wall painting created in the seventeenth-century by an Armenian school of artists; the fresco was in the church of Saint Saviour, in Djoulfa, Middle East. The horrors of hell are here graphically defined, and the more shocking for the arch-realism of their portrayal. The scene bristles with pointed horns, jagged teeth and the sharp corners of the instruments of torture wielded by the demons – by turn staring-eyed, as if bored, then furiously vindictive. Their anthropomorphic bodies mingle with those of the damned whom they torture; their very physical intimacy contributing to the revulsion the scene was designed to inspire. The horrified expression – and quasi decapitated head – of this woman is echoed by the numerous other suffering souls in the fresco, the sight of whose agony is more atrocious than the flames in which they writhe.

ABOVE: This painted miniature from a French manuscript of the late fifteenth century depicts Pluto and Persephone, rulers of the classical underworld, seated on their throne with the three-headed dog Cerberus docile at their feet. The work, an allegorical romance entitled *Les Échecs Amoureux*, was made *c* 1496–8 for Louise de Savoie; its author was Evrart de Conty and the illuminator Robinet Testart. Unusually, the god and goddess of the underworld are depicted as an aged couple (Persephone is a ghastly crone, incongruous in her graceful, veiled henin; Pluto is darkly haggard). Both are listening to what appears to be a civilized concert, played by two elegant ladies on a harp and rebec (a violin-type instrument of Middle-Eastern origin). In this context, the red figures on the left could almost pass for courtiers, were it not for the demons with horns and unnatural breasts on the right, who are torturing the human figures – to the tune, presumably, of a diabolic score.

OPPOSITE (BELOW): A fresco image of Satan in the depths of hell, attributed to the Italian artist Vitale da Bologna (*c* 1308–60). As with many other representations of hell of the period, Satan is shown devouring the damned, body and soul (in Dante's *Inferno* a three-faced Satan gobbles up the souls of the traitors Judas Iscariot, Judas and Brutus). Likewise, physically as well as spiritually, the damned are presented as disjointed – literally disembodied – and fragmented, while the saved in Last Judgement representations are shown as whole; it was not surprising, then, that hell was most often depicted as a mouth that swallows the damned.

RIGHT: A sixteenth-century illustration of Dante's *Divine Comedy* (1321) showing Satan devouring the soul of Judas Iscariot, who betrayed Christ and thus set in train the events that would lead to the Crucifixion. In Dante's *Inferno*, the ninth circle of hell is at the centre of the earth; it is where Satan – the Great Worm in the earth's core – is to be found. Dante describes Satan as having three faces, each of a different colour (red for hatred; yellow for impotence; and black for ignorance). Each one devours an infamous sinner: the middle face chews Judas Iscariot, while the other two faces can be seen devouring Cassius and Brutus, the principal assassins of Julius Caesar. Around Satan are half-submerged souls in the icy waters of Lake Cocytus.

The Rout of Evil

One notable aspect of the belief in demons in the Middle Ages was the frequency of images of saints fending off temptations – of the flesh, the lure of worldly riches or temporal power – as well as doing battle with 'the dragon, that old serpent' (Revelation 20:1) – the Devil himself. Images of the latter commonly depicted Saint Michael, the Devil's chief adversary and champion of God's people, as the victorious slayer of evil. Textual sources for the routing of evil by saints existed in the many edifying accounts of their lives – hermit saints like Anthony (who overcame demons with aggressive bestial likenesses as well as in the shape of alluring female beauties), female saints like Margaret of Antioch, Catherine of Siena and Mary Magdalene (a penitent sinner), and Saint Francis of Assisi. Also popular was the theme of rescue from peril by the Madonna, or Virgin Mary. In all of these encounters, demons are readily overcome by those whom God has chosen.

In their battles with the Devil and his provocations, the saints were seen to be reliving Christ's battle with the Devil as recounted in the gospels of Matthew, Mark and Luke, each of whom tells how, at the end of his 40-day fast in the desert, Christ was thrice confronted by the Devil. First, Satan tempted Christ to turn stones into bread to prove he was the Son of God. Then Satan bid Christ cast himself off a parapet of the Temple, so that angels might break his fall. Finally, Satan took Christ to a pinnacle overlooking the kingdoms of the world, promising dominion over them all if he would fall down and pay Satan homage. Each time, Christ repudiated Satan with quotations from the Scriptures: 'Man shall not live by bread alone' (Luke 4: 4); 'It is written . . . Thou shalt not tempt the Lord thy God' (Matthew 4:7); 'Thou shalt worship the Lord thy God, and him only shalt thou serve' (Matthew 4:10; Luke 4:8). The example of Christ withstanding the assaults of the Tempter provided a perfect model of resistance for the faithful.

Another scene popular with the early Church was the episode, based on an apocryphal gospel, of Christ's descent into Limbo – also known as the 'harrowing of hell' (harrow in this context means 'to ravage'). The traditional imagery shows Satan being trampled underfoot, his demons fleeing into the darkness, as Christ breaks open the gates of hell to liberate the souls of the Old Testament saints. Exorcism, of course, was another powerful example of the expulsion of evil, and again, images of saints and bishops routing demons recalled gospel episodes in which Christ banished demons.

Such images of the triumph over evil provided proof, if proof were needed, that the agents of Satan could be overcome with Christian armour – the Cross, and the Word of God as revealed in the Scriptures. The theme of the 'moment of trial' in the lives of the faithful would endure well beyond medieval times – indeed, the idea of the soul's struggle was a key motif of Counter-Reformation imagery – recurring in depictions of episodes from saints' lives for centuries after.

ABOVE: *Saint George Vanquishes the Dragon* by an unknown Lombard master active in the middle of the fifteenth century. Today the painting is in the Pinacoteca Tosio Martinengo, Brescia, Italy. One version of his legend has it that George was born in Cappadocia, Asia Minor in the third century, a city he was said to have rescued from paganism. In early Christian iconography, the saved Cappodocia was represented by a lady, while the dragon represented paganism. The origins of this symbolism were forgotten over time, and it was given a new interpretation in the thirteenth-century *Legenda Aurea* (or *Golden Legend*). In that work, Saint George kills the dragon to save the princess, who had been offered as a sacrifice to the creature that was lurking outside the city walls. Here, Saint George – on a white charger (for purity) and dressed as a courtly medieval knight – lances the dragon while, in the background, the citizens of the city look on.

OPPOSITE: *Saint George and the Dragon* by an unknown artist, School of the higher Rhine, fifteenth century. The painting is in the Louvre, Paris, France. Little is known about the real Saint George. The *Catholic Encyclopedia* cautions readers to remember 'the unscrupulous freedom with which any wild story, even when pagan in origin, was appropriated by the early hagiographers to the honour of a popular saint' and warns that 'we are fairly safe in assuming that the Acts of Saint George, though ancient in date and preserved to us (with endless variations) in many different languages, afford absolutely no indication at all for arriving at the saint's authentic history'. However, it continues, this 'by no means implies that the martyr Saint George never existed. An ancient cultus, going back to a very early epoch and connected with a definite locality, in itself constitutes a strong historical argument'. Whatever the historical basis for the various legends of Saint George, the saint was venerated in England in the eighth century, and became popular throughout Europe at the time of the first crusades in the eleventh century; by the fifteenth century Saint George's Day was as important in England as Christmas Day.

ABOVE: *Saint Michael Killing the Dragon*, an oil on panel by Josse Lieferinxe, also known as the Master of Saint Sebastian (*c* 1493–1508). A horned, beaked and taloned dragon is overcome with consummate ease by a graceful and elegantly attired Saint Michael, who boasts swan-like wings and bears the scales of justice and the banner of the Resurrection. Works by Lieferinxe, who was active in Marseilles in the south of France during the reign of the cultured provençal King Réné, are often grouped under the banner of the 'School of Avignon'. This panel, with its bold colouring and simple geometric volumes, shows the happy marriage of Italian delicacy and Flemish emotional expressivity that this particular style could achieve.

SAINTE MARGUERITE A CHARTRE.CIE

ABOVE: Saint Margaret of Antioch trampling a dragon; a nineteenth-century illustration. Saint Margaret is shown holding a palm frond, which was an attribute of martyrdom and, in the Middle Ages, a symbol of chastity. According to legend, Margaret was born in Antioch, Asia Minor, in the fourth century. Disowned by her father, a pagan priest, when she embraced Christianity, she later attracted the lustful attentions of the Roman prefect Olybrius. Spurning his interest and ignoring his order to abandon her faith on pain of death, Olybrius first tried to have her burnt and then – when the flames had no effect – ordered her to be bound and gagged and thrown into a cauldron of boiling water. In answer to Margaret's prayers she emerged unscathed and, finally, Olybrius ordered her to be beheaded. Saint Margaret is sometimes shown leading a chained dragon (symbol of Satan and, for early Christians, paganism in particular) and standing by a cauldron. Here the dragon cowers at her feet.

RIGHT: Saint Dunstan and the Devil; an illustration (possibly by George Cruikshank) in William Hone's *The Every-Day Book*. Born (probably early in the tenth century) near Glastonbury, Somerset, Dunstan became Archbishop of Canterbury in 961. He was the patron saint of the goldsmiths' guild in the Middle Ages and the illustration refers to the eleventh-century legend that, when interrupted while making a golden chalice, Dunstan seized the Devil by the nose with red-hot pincers and refused to release him until he promised never to tempt Dunstan again. The illustration featured in William Hone's highly successful *The Every-Day Book*, which was an extraordinary collection of miscellaneous knowledge, anecdotes, facts, biographic and historical sketches (including saints' lives), and even gardening tips and observations on aspects of folklore. The book began appearing in instalments in January, 1825; the instalments were published in book form in 1826 and 1827.

ABOVE: *Satan Chained to a Rock* by an unknown Italian artist in the fifteenth century. Apart from talons on his feet and hands and the lies, like fire, that he spews, Satan here appears like a normal, weak human; such a depiction would have reminded the viewer of the composite nature of the Devil, as 'old serpent' and false prophet. The main reference to the chaining of Satan in the canonical scriptures was in Revelation: 'And I saw an angel come down from heaven, having the key of the bottomless pit and a great chain in his hand. And he laid hold on the dragon, that old serpent, which is the Devil, and Satan, and bound him a thousand years' (Revelation 20:1–3); in the Apocryphal Gospel of Nicodemus, which was possibly written in the fourth century, Christ binds Satan in chains after the harrowing of hell and having released the Old Testament prophets and patriarchs. This subject became a popular one in medieval drama and literature. Later, in his *Paradise Lost* (which was first published in 1667), Milton refers to the 'Arch-fiend' Satan 'stretcht out huge in length . . . Chain'd on the burning Lake' (*Paradise Lost*, I, 210).

RIGHT: *Saint Michael and Saint Engracia*, a late fifteenth-century painting by the Spanish (Aragonian) artist Juan de la Abadia. Saint Michael stands on the Devil; in his right hand he holds the scales that he uses to weigh the souls of men. To his left is Saint Engracia (also sometimes Encratis or Encratide), a virgin martyred *c* 304 at Saragossa in Spain. The martyr reputedly survived various tortures, but died when she was sent back to prison; however, she is not among Prudentius' list of 18 martyrs who died in Saragossa during the Emperor Diocletian's persecutions of the Christians in the early years of the fourth century. In one hand, Saint Engracia holds a martyr's palm and a nail protrudes from her head. The latter may symbolize Christ's Passion; it certainly indicates the method of Saint Engracia's martyrdom – depictions of martyrs frequently depicted the instrument of torture and/or death, such as an arrow or vat of oil.

OPPOSITE: *Christ in Limbo,* by Martin Schöngauer (c 1450–91). The painting, which dates from about 1480, is in the Unterlinden Museum, Colmar, France. After his Crucifixion, Christ descends into hell to rescue Old Testament prophets, patriarchs, forefathers and martyrs. Here Christ, who shows signs of his recent Crucifixion and holds the banner of the Resurrection (a red cross on a white background), has smashed through the gates of hell, trapping various demons under the debris while others flee in terror. Adam and Eve emerge first, Adam clasping Jesus' hands in thanks; John the Baptist (by pillar, with beard) looks on in wonder, while other Old Testament figures applaud. According to medieval theology, the Old Testament patriarchs were in Limbo because they lived in the time before Jesus, and so were denied the possibility of Salvation. There was much debate about whether Limbo was actually in hell, or indeed whether it was a real place or a temporal dimension: to the early Fathers of the Church this netherworld (the term 'limbo' was not used in this precise context until the twelfth century) was on hell's borders, while in Dante's *Inferno* it formed the first circle of hell.

ABOVE: The Harrowing of Hell; an English alabaster carving of the fifteenth century depicting Christ's Descent into Limbo, when He 'harrows' – ravages or despoils – that place. On His arrival in Limbo, according to the apocryphal Gospel of Nicodemus, 'the Saviour blessed Adam upon his forehead with the sign of the cross' before 'leap[ing] up out of hell' with Adam and the other Old Testament prophets and forefathers. Here the entrance to hell is shown as Leviathan's mouth – even though there was much debate about whether Limbo was actually in hell, or indeed a physical place at all.

The Rout of Evil 181

ABOVE: Christ calms the storm and casts out the devils; a page from the *Holkham Bible Picture Book*. The page describes two miraculous events recounted by Luke in chapter 8 (22–39). First, when Christ, having fallen asleep while crossing Galilee with the disciples, is woken by them when a storm threatens their safety; Christ calms the storm, causing the disciples to ask each other: 'What manner of man is this! For he commandeth even the winds and water, and they obey him' (Luke 8: 25). The second event occurs when, having arrived on the other side of Galilee, Jesus and the disciples meet a man, 'which had devils long time'. Jesus casts out the devils and they enter a nearby herd of swine, 'and the herd ran violently down a steep place into the lake, and were choked' (8: 33). The *Holkham Bible Picture Book* was created in the fourteenth century and was kept at Holkham in Norfolk until it was transferred to the British Library, London. The Book, which incorporates much apocryphal material and recounts key events from the Bible, would have been used as an instructional aid by a preacher on his visits to wealthy merchants.

LEFT: *Fall of the Rebel Angels* (1562) by Pieter Bruegel (*c* 1525–69). The expelled Rebel Angels tumble chaotically from the halo-shaped light of Heaven at the top of the painting towards a dark, cavern-like hell, aided on their way by graceful Angels. As they plummet, their appearance changes to reveal their true, corrupt nature. Meanwhile, their commander, Saint Michael, strikes the dragon (who represents Satan) at the very centre of the picture. In his depiction of the fall of the Rebel Angels, Bruegel harks back to the imagery of Hieronymus Bosch: the screaming mass of animal, insect and human hybrid monsters creates a sense of a seething, tumultuous and disordered hell where there will be neither rest nor silence.

ABOVE: Saint Bernard of Menthon (923–1008) depicted overcoming a demon, from a fifteenth-century Book of Hours. Born in Menthon, near Annecy, in Savoy, Bernard founded hospices for travellers in the high Alps (in the Great Saint Bernard and Little Saint Bernard passes). This image, on vellum, relates to a legend which was in circulation even during the saint's lifetime. According to this, Bernard and a group of pilgrims climbed a mountain where a brigand, Procus, was being worshipped as a pagan god, and where a monstrous dragon lay ready to devour the band. Bernard made the sign of the Cross and threw his priest's stole over the monster's neck, whereupon the garment was transformed into a chain. The pilgrims killed the dragon, and the silken ends of the stole that remained in the saint's hands were long preserved in the abbey of Saint Maurice-en-Valais.

OPPOSITE: The archangel Uriel tricked by Satan; an illustration from a nineteenth-century edition of John Milton's *Paradise Lost* (1667). In the poem Milton describes how, having resolved to avenge God for casting him out of Heaven, Satan sets out on a journey to find, and then corrupt, God's creations: the world and mankind. Here, Satan has arrived at the sun and, by disguising himself as a cherub, has tricked the unsuspecting Uriel – Milton's 'Regent of the Sun' – into showing him the way.

OPPOSITE: A bishop carrying out an exorcism; a fifteenth-century woodcut illustration. In his book *Demons*, Anthony Finlay writes that 'for early Christians encounters with and experience of both angels and demons, psychically and actually, were not thought unusual. For them the invisible world was a reality'. By the fifteenth century, the awareness of the supposed reality of demonic activity in everyday life had developed into an almost obsessive fear of demons and their doings, among clergy and people alike. In 1486 the infamous *Malleus Maleficarum* ('Hammer of the Witches') was published, for example, giving precise instructions on how to discover, try and punish witches. The book was immensely successful; it not only became, in Finlay's words, a 'second Bible for inquisitors and witch-finders' throughout Europe, but also opened the gates 'to many [other] treatises on demonology and witchcraft in the following century or so'. The obsession of the Church and general population with sorcery reached its zenith in the sixteenth century and continued into the seventeenth.

ABOVE: A priest exorcising a woman; a thirteenth century bronze panel from the door of the Church of San Zeno Maggiore, Verona, Italy. The horrified demon leaves the body of the possessed woman, while the officiating priest sprays holy water on her with an aspergillum (a short-handled brush used by Catholic priests to sprinkle holy water on communicants during Mass). Like many other Christian depictions of exorcisms over the centuries, this image emphasizes the authoritative stance and demeanour of the priest and the extraordinary, almost uncontrollable strength of the possessed person (here, the priest's assistant has to grasp the woman's arm firmly to hold her still, while the priest calmly continues with his work). It was also usual to depict the demon leaving the possessed via the mouth, as well as to portray the demon itself as a miniature version of Satan.

ABOVE: *Saint Philip Exorcising a Demon* (also known as *Philip the Apostle in the Temple of Mars*), *c* 1497–1500, a fresco by Filippino Lippi in the church of Santa Maria Novella, Florence, Italy. *The Golden Legend* told how Philip the Apostle was captured by pagans in Scythia, who took him to the Temple of Mars (the Roman god is shown on a column with a wolf, one of his attributes), where they tried to make him give sacrificial offerings to the pagan god of war. This fresco was faithful to the popular story. It shows the Devil in the shape of a dragon appearing at the foot of the idol, his 'corrupted breath' infecting those assembled and even killing some of them with its lethal stench. Philip commands the people to replace the idol with the Cross, with the promise that in so doing all those present would be revived – even those now lying dead. In the tale, the Devil departed and Philip healed the sick and raised the dead, afterwards baptizing them all.

OPPOSITE: *Saint Michael and the Devil* (1956–8) by Sir Jacob Epstein (1880–1959). In November, 1940, Saint Michael's Cathedral, Coventry was largely destroyed in a bombing raid; after the War, the competition to design a new cathedral was won by Basil Spence. Leading British artists, including John Piper, Graham Sutherland and Elisabeth Frink, as well as the American-born Epstein, all contributed work to the new cathedral, which was consecrated in 1962. Epstein's enormous bronze statue – it weighs four tons and is some six metres in height – guards the entrance to the new cathedral. Because the entrance is positioned between the nave of the new building and the remains of the old Cathedral, Epstein's Saint Michael forcefully completes the narrative of destruction and resurrection, of the inevitability of the triumph of good over evil, that the eye of the visitor 'reads' from left to right as he or she approaches the new Saint Michael's.

OPPOSITE: The Virgin Mary rescuing souls from demons; an illustration from *The Miracles of the Blessed Virgin Mary and the Life of Hannâ*. An Ethiopian illuminated manuscript c 1670–80, the book described various miracles attributed to the Virgin Mary, as well as giving the life-story of Saint Anne (*Hannâ*), the Virgin's mother, and including a selection of 'Magical Prayers'. The highly stylized composition shows a woman (centre) reporting the rescue to a senior scribe (centre, left), who records the miracle in his manuscript; this is then copied by junior scribes (seated below). The blue-robed, haloed Mary dominates the scene, wresting one soul by its foot from the grasp of one of the heavy-set, dark-skinned demons.

ABOVE: Sculpture in the abbey at Souillac, France, depicting the Devil giving the pact to Theophilus, the Devil dragging the monk away, and the pact being taken to Heaven by the Virgin Mary. Theophilus was an Archdeacon in Adana, Cicilia (modern Turkey) in the sixth century; when offered the bishopric he declined it, but when the bishop appointed in his place ejected him from his post Theophilus became so angry he made a pact with the Devil and vowed to renounce Christ and the Virgin in return for preferment. Later, regretting what he had done, Theophilus prayed to the Virgin who, after interceding with God, granted him absolution for his sin. The Devil was not willing to release Theophilus from the pact, however, and, as a reminder of what had been agreed, placed the pact on Theophilus' chest one morning so he would find it when he woke. Realising there was only one way to escape the Devil's clutches, Theophilus publicly confessed to what he had done; in one of the many versions of the legend he then expired from relief at being released from the pact. The legend of Theophilus is the oldest story concerning a pact with the Devil; it served as the inspiration for later developments by Christopher Marlowe and Goethe of the Faust story.

OPPOSITE: Christian meets Apollyon; an engraving of an illustration by W M Craig in a nineteenth-century edition of John Bunyan's *Pilgrim's Progess*. After leaving the Palace Beautiful while on his journey from the City of Destruction to the Celestial City on Mount Zion, Christian meets the monster Apollyon. Lord of the City of Destruction (which is, as Christian calls it, 'the place of all evil'), 'the destroyer' (as Christian calls Apollyon) is 'hideous to behold: he was clothed with scales like a fish, and they are his pride; he had wings like a dragon, and feet like a bear, and out of his belly came fire and smoke; and his mouth was as the mouth of a lion'. Apollyon tries to persuade Christian to abandon the path of Faith and, when he refuses, fires flaming darts at him; Christian and Satan's 'Prince' fight for half a day, until Christian draws his sword and, aided by 'blessed Michael' (Saint Michael), mortally wounds Apollyon. Bunyan's great Christian allegory was first published in 1678; an expanded edition was published a year later and Part Two, which describes the journey of Christian's wife Christiana and their sons to the Celestial City, was published in 1684.

ABOVE: The Rout of Satan; an illustration from a late twelfth-century English Psalter. Satan tumbles towards hell, with a look of anguish on his second face, while Christ looks on. Popular in the early Middle Ages, Psalters contained the 150 psalms, together with other devotional material such as a calendar, litany of saints and canticles from the Old and New Testaments. Psalters were used both at home and in church and were particularly popular with lay-people, but were supplanted in the thirteenth century by Books of Hours. Divided into eight sections (or 'Hours') designed to be read at specific times of each day, these contained hymns, prayers, lessons from the Gospels and other material (depending on the owner's taste and requirements), as well as the psalms.

RIGHT: *The Temptation of Saint Anthony by Wild Beasts*; a seventeenth-century painting by an unknown artist. Following the death of his parents when he was a young man in Coma, Upper Egypt, Anthony (*c* 251–356) sold his possessions, distributed the proceeds among the poor and retreated to the desert. He lived a solitary, ascetic life there for many years, and suffered terrible temptations by demons. These took many forms, but it is his temptation by monsters and wild animals (which attack him) or his visions of beautiful women (who are often shown nude in paintings from the sixteenth century onwards) that are depicted most often in Christian art, together with his visit to Saint Paul the Hermit. The theme of Saint Anthony's temptations has fascinated artists over the years, from Bosch (*c* 1450–1516) and David Teniers the Younger (1610–90) to Cézanne (1839–1906) and Salvador Dali (1904–89). The saint is usually shown as an old, bearded man; he wears a monk's cowl and habit, signifying his role as the founder of monasticism.

LEFT: *The Temptation of Christ by Satan*; an illustration from a book of 1531. Matthew (4: 1–11) and Luke (41–13) both describe how, at the end of His 40 days in the desert, Jesus is tempted three times by Satan. First, he challenges Christ to turn stones into bread, then (in Matthew) Satan takes Jesus to the pinnacle of the temple in Jerusalem and invites Him to cast Himself down to see if God will send angels to save him; finally, Satan shows Jesus many lands from the top of a mountain and promises Him 'All these things … if thou wilt fall down and worship me' (Matthew 4:9). Here, the main scene shows the first temptation. The other two temptations are shown in the background (left, second temptation; right, final temptation). The illustration shows how medieval artists stressed Satan's evil nature through his appearance: he is a monstrous hybrid, with feet like a chicken's, a hairy middle like a satyr's (with a tail and second face for good measure) while the hooded eyes, overly large mouth and misformed nose of his main face give him a duplicitous, deceitful air. Jesus, by contrast, stands in an authoritative posture; His features are fine and His hair is neatly arranged.

ABOVE: *The Temptation of Christ by Satan*; an illustration from the *Isabella Breviary*. In the foreground, Satan tempts Christ to turn the stones into bread, while in the background (top left) he tempts Christ from the highest mountain and from the pinnacle of the Temple in Jerusalem (right). Satan has disguised himself as a monk, even carrying Rosary beads, in an attempt to deceive Christ. However, his horns peep through his hood and, in the main scene, Christ's gestures warn him away. The *Isabella Breviary* was written and illuminated in Flanders, probably at Bruges (today in Belgium), during the last decade of the fifteenth century; it was presented by Francisco de Roias to Queen Isabella in about 1497 and is now in the British Library, London, England.

OPPOSITE: *The Madonna del Soccorso Saves a Boy from Satan,* possibly by Cosimo Rosselli (1439–1507). The painting on wood is in the Church of San Spirito, Florence, Italy, which was designed by architect Filippo Brunelleschi (1337–1446). The Madonna del Soccorso reputedly first appeared to Nicolo Bruno, an Augustinian monk, in 1300 in Sciacca, Italy. Bruno was lying in bed, suffering from fevers and a broken neck, when the Madonna appeared to in a vision and cured him. Further miracles were attributed to the Madonna in the town, including the one depicted here. According to the legend, the mother (left) of a six-year-old-boy, driven to distraction by his naughtiness, shouted at him to 'go to the devil', at which point Satan appeared to take the boy away. Realising her error, the mother appealed to the Madonna del Soccorso to save the boy. The Madonna duly appeared, carrying a club which she used to knock Satan to the ground. The boy then ran to the Madonna (as portrayed here) and hid under her cape. After trampling on Satan and before disappearing, the Madonna is reputed to have had turned to the mother and said: 'Put your trust in the Madonna del Soccorso, for I am the Protector of Sciacca'.

ABOVE: *The Madonna del Soccorso Saving a Boy from Satan* (c 1506) by Giovanni Pagani (c 1465–1544). The painting, which is now in the Louvre, Paris, France, was completed in about 1506 – slightly later than the picture shown on the left attributed to Cosimo Rosselli. Although this depiction of the Madonna del Soccorso's miraculous intervention sets the scene outside the mother and child's home, other details are similar, from the posture and larger-than-life size of the Madonna to the mother's expression and gestures. Here, however, the Devil is black and, although his wings are also dragon-like, his body is mainly hairless, not furred like a satyr's. The extravagant growth of wiry, tangled hair on this devil's lower stomach and groin is a startling detail lacking in the earlier painting: it emphasizes the devil's animal carnality, lending him a far more menacing presence than the slightly smaller devil of the painting attributed to Cosimo Rosselli.

The Rout of Evil | 201

ABOVE: A demon threatens the life of a sailor, whose vessel has been caught in a storm possibly raised by the demon itself; an illustration from *Le Grand Calendrier et Compost des Bergers*. The text accompanying the illustration draws an analogy between the human soul's journey through life and the ship's voyage across unpredictable, storm-tossed seas with its precious cargo; its destination port is 'paradise', beyond a sea of 'vice and sins'. The sailor (whose 'precious cargo' is his own soul) would rather reach home safely than risk life and limb for material riches. God, holding an orb, looks down from above, and the text ends with a prayer of thanks to the 'Lord who watches over us'. *Le Grand Calendrier* was an almanac of religious, moral and astrological advice. First published in France in 1491, it was reprinted many times and was still in circulation 300 years later. It purported to teach the 'science of the shepherds [which is the] science of the soul, body, stars, life and death.'

ABOVE: Saints Cosmas and Damian Saved from Drowning; a devotional panel painted between 1438 and 1440 by Fra Angelico. This was one of the nine predella panels of the altarpiece in the chapel of the Convent of San Marco, Florence, Italy. The Dominican convent, which was constructed in 1436 at the behest of Cosimo de Medici the Elder (1389–1464), was dedicated to the physicians and martyrs, Cosmas and Damian. Born in Arabia, the two Christians would accept no money for their healing work; when Diocletian's persecutions began, they refused to recant their faith, and were tortured by submersion in water, by burning, and on the cross; they were miraculously saved each time and were finally beheaded. All but the main panel and central predella panel of the San Marco altarpiece showed scenes from their lives: the healing of Palladia; the two saints before Diocletian's prefect, Lisius; their condemnation and burning; their crucifixion and stoning; their beheading; their entombment; and their healing of Saint Justinian (the Emperor Justinian I, 527–65, who had been cured of an illness by the saints' miraculous intercession). The main panel depicted the Virgin and Child and the central predella panel, the Entombment of Christ (Pietà). The altarpiece was broken up and the panels dispersed in the seventeenth century; this section is now in the Alte Pinakothek, Munich, Germany.

LEFT: Job tormented by devils; from a French Book of Hours, *c* 1500. In the Old Testament Book of Job, Job's faith is tried by Satan, with the permission of God (Yahweh), who here looks down on the scene. Job bears six great temptations with patience; his last and greatest trial comes when he is visited by his friends Eliphaz, Bildad and Zophar, who state that they believe Job's trials must be punishment for some wrongdoing. Job protests that his sufferings are undeserved and, moreover, that experience of this world proves that the wicked often triumph while the good suffer. However, although he remarks on the seemingly unjust severity of God in punishing the good for even the smallest wrongdoings, Job never questions His ultimate righteousness or authority: he keeps to his Faith and Satan fails in his attempt to break it. Eliu, a youth listening to the arguments, is then inspired to recognize that suffering is not always the result of sin: it can also, he argues, be a sign of God's love for humankind, in that it is the way by which He tries, and promotes, virtue. God himself confirms the veracity of this perception and, in the Epilogue, both affirms Job's innocence and restores him to double his former prosperity.

OPPOSITE: Christ's Descent into Limbo; a fourteenth-century altarpiece. In this depiction of Christ's Harrowing of Hell, Leviathan's mouth and head – with its staring red eyes and sharply pointed teeth – dominate. Horned demons watch as Christ, assisted by angels, leads Adam (first, as was usual in such scenes), Eve, and other Old Testament figures out of Limbo. There is no absolutely clear scriptural basis for the belief that Christ descended into Limbo after his Crucifixion, although in Ephesians Paul talks of Him 'descend[ing] first into the lower parts of the earth' (4:9) before ascending into Heaven, as does the Apostle's Creed, which (in the form in which it is known today) probably dates from the second half of the fifth century. However, non-scriptural texts describing the event were in circulation by the second century and, in about the fourth-century, the apocryphal Gospel of Nicodemus recounted the story in full for the first time. The story given in Nicodemus was then repeated in the thirteenth-century *Legenda Aurea* (*Golden Legend*).

ABOVE: An angel binds Satan in chains; a miniature from a twelfth-century commentary on the Apocalypse. The scene referred to in the illustration is Revelation 20: 1–3, where Satan is described as 'the dragon, that old serpent'. The angel is shown holding the keys to 'the bottomless pit' (hell), where Satan will be bound for 1,000 years. The figure in the stocks-like contraption may be the Anti-Christ. Although Revelation describes the latter as a beast with seven heads and ten horns, medieval Apocalypse commentaries often depicted the Anti-Christ as human in form. This reflected medieval interpretations of Apocalyptic texts: 'Antichrist will be a single human, a man with devilish connections who will come near the end of the world to persecute Christians and to mislead them by claiming that he is Christ …' (R K Emmerson: *Antichrist in the Middle Ages*). Significantly, this humanoid creature clearly has some of the attributes of the Anti-Christ, as described in Revelation (13:2): he has leopard-like spots, and his feet are 'as the feet of a bear'.

ABOVE: *The Expulsion of the Demons from Arezzo*, a fresco (c 1295–1300) by Giotto di Bondone in the Upper Church of San Francesco, Assisi, Italy. This is the tenth of 28 frescoes in the Upper Church all of which depict scenes from Saint Francis' life; all but three of the scenes were painted by Giotto. This scene refers to the legend that, during the civil war in Arezzo, Saint Francis called on a fellow monk, Sylvester, to rid the city of the demons that he had seen over it. Here, both are outside the city walls; the discord that has plagued the city is represented by the large crack that separates it from its surroundings. While the haloed Saint Francis prays, Sylvester commands the demons to leave; as they flee into the sky, the citizens wait, peering from the city's gates, ready to return to normal life. Giotto changed the course of European painting, heralding the move towards a new and distinct Renaissance style. The Arezzo frescoes are among the most important of his works.

OPPOSITE: *The Triumphant Messiah*, an 1802 painting by Heinrich Füssli (1741–1825). In the first part of John Milton's *Paradise Lost* (1667), the Archangel Raphael tells Adam about Lucifer's rebellion against God, describing how he leaves Heaven with a third of all the angels on the day that God announces his Son as his successor. The form Satan takes (Raphael tells Adam that 'his former name [Lucifer]/Is heard no more in Heaven') changes over the course of the poem, reflecting his moral degradation: initially, as here, he is powerful and handsome but, as his true nature becomes apparent, he appears in increasingly debased forms: as a cherub, a cormorant, a toad and, finally, a snake. A Swiss-born painter, draughtsman and writer on art, Fuseli (as he began spelling his name when he moved to England in 1765) became one of the leading figures of the Romantic movement and a friend of William Blake's. He was fascinated by the grotesque and by the murky workings of the subconscious mind.

RIGHT: The mouth of hell, with sinners released by Christ. An engraving of 1561 commissioned by the publisher Hieronymus Cock from a drawing by Pieter Bruegel the Elder (c 1525–69). Here, Christ (centre, in a sphere of purity with his angels), has, as if miraculously, descended into hell to release the Old Testament prophets, patriarchs and forefathers from Limbo, who stream through the gates, now smashed, that had kept them within Leviathan's mouth (left). In his depiction of hell, Bruegel was clearly influenced by Hieronymus Bosch, whose works were much-imitated, and who was very popular, at the time. However, although Bruegel borrowed some of Bosch's imagery (the grotesque hybrids, for example) his inventiveness of detail in other respects means this picture transcends mere imitation. Bruegel's hell, for example, appears as a sort of charnel-house, where some kind of ghastly rendering process is systematically carried out on the tormented souls consigned to it. Naked, physically complete bodies (presumably recently judged souls) tumble from above onto the wheel device, then via a chute to be further 'processed' in the cauldron-like contraption with two legs; from there they emerge – either in the form of a grotesque, or physically incomplete, like the headless man – onto the floor of the 'factory'. On the near side of the black, Saintyx-like river the souls are tormented further by various grotesque creatures.

OPPOSITE: King David Penitent, by Jean Fouquet, painted *c* 1452–61 for the *Hours of Etienne Chevalier*, one of the most lavishly illustrated illuminated manuscripts of the fifteenth century. The brightly coloured devils subject the damned to the tortures of hell while what may be plague victims await burial. David is in fashionable Renaissance armour, and kneels in supplication to God, who is enthroned among cherubim and seraphim. According to medieval tradition, David was the author of the seven penitential psalms, which he reputedly wrote to atone for his sins, which included committing adultery, murdering Uriah (by proxy) and pride. For committing the latter sin God gave David (and Israel) the choice of suffering plague, hunger or war. David accepted the latter penalty with such grace that he was forgiven, while the sincerity of his penitence led to his adoption by the church and artists as a model and symbol for all penitents.

ABOVE: Satan clasping David; an illustration from an undated medieval illuminated manuscript. Born in Bethlehem in *c* 1085 BC, David became a shepherd and then King of Israel, reigning from 1055 to 1015 BC. A great soldier and leader, he defeated Goliath, forged a united, independent Israel and, capturing Jerusalem, made it the nation's capital and religious centre. Drawing parallels between the life of David and Jesus (for example, Jesus was the Good Shepherd and a leader of men, like David; both were born in Bethlehem), the Church Fathers saw David as a prefiguration, or 'type', of Christ – an identification encouraged by both Matthew and Luke in their Gospels (Matthew 1:1, refers to Jesus as 'son of David'). David's slaying of Goliath, meanwhile, was taken to prefigure Christ's temptation in the wilderness – David slew the Philistine's champion just as Jesus defeated Satan, in refusing the latter's temptations. Here, the righteous King David, sword of faith, truth and justice firmly to the fore, resists Satan's blandishments.

ABOVE: Saint George Defeats the Dragon; an undated illustration, possibly from a copy of the thirteenth-century *Legenda Aurea* (*Golden Legend*). After reputedly appearing to aid the Crusaders at the Battle of Antioch in 1098, Saint George was adopted as the patron saint of soldiers and, later, England's King Richard I (1157–99) put his entire Crusading army under the protection of Saint George. The Irish patriot and author Michael Collins (1890–1922) notes that, around the same time that Saint George was made Patron Saint of England by Edward, 'the banner of Saint George, the red cross on a white background, was adopted for the uniform of English soldiers possibly in the reign of Richard I . . . [and] in 1348, George was adopted by King Edward III [1239–1307] as Principal Patron of his new order of Chivalry, the Knights of the Garter'. Here, Saint George is depicted as a chivalrous knight, fearlessly stabbing the dragon in the mouth with his lance.

ABOVE: *Saint George and the Dragon* by Paolo Uccello (1397–1475); the picture, which today is in the National Gallery, London, was painted in about 1470. It shows two episodes from the story of Saint George as told in the *Legenda Aurea* (or *Golden Legend*), a highly popular (and much-translated) collection of saints' lives written between 1260 and 1275 by Jacobus de Voragine (*c* 1231–98), Archbishop of Genoa. The first episode describes the saint's defeat of a plague-bearing dragon that had been terrorizing a city; in the second, the rescued princess uses her belt as a leash to bring the dragon to heel. Uccello had developed a profound interest in perspective and composition in the 1430s and that passion is apparent here, for example in the way in which the eye of the gathering storm lines up with Saint George's lance (this alignment suggests that divine intervention has helped him to victory over the beast) and also in the almost formal arrangement of the patches of grass.

RIGHT: Saint George Vanquishes the Dragon; an illustration dating from *c* 1500. Saint George here is depicted as the ideal chivalrous knight; the meekly abject dragon is little more than a prop, compared with the ferocious and deadly symbol of evil and paganism of earlier representations, as seen elsewhere in this chapter. The same applies to the lady Saint George has saved: she is barely visible in the background. With his beautifully crafted black armour and fashionable hat (which sits comfortably undisturbed even though the presumably ferocious battle with the dragon has only just ended), it is the courtly demeanour and dress of Saint George himself, not the elemental battle between paganism and Christianity, good and evil, that is the true subject of this painting.

ABOVE: *Christ's Descent into Limbo* (*c* 1450) by Fra Angelico (*c* 1387–1455). The fresco can still be seen in the Museo di San Marco, Florence, Italy. As in some of the other depictions of Christ's Harrowing of Hell which can be seen elsewhere in this chapter, Christ has smashed the doors to hell, trapping a demon underneath; while other demons cower in the shadows, cracks appear in the stone and light flows in from behind Christ. Christ carries the banner of the Resurrection and reaches out to Adam who is followed by John the Baptist, Eve and Noah. Unlike in other, earlier, depictions of the scene, all the rescued patriarchs, forefathers and prophets are haloed. This reflects developments in thinking at the time concerning whether or not those Old Testament figures who had died before the time of Christ had suffered while they were in what Saint Peter called the 'prison' (I Peter 3:19) in the 'lower parts of the earth' (Ephesians 4:9). For it was only in the twelfth century that Peter Lombard and subsequently Pope Innocent III rejected Saint Augustine's belief that even those guilty only of original sin suffered in misery, teaching instead that such souls suffered no physical or spiritual pain, but only the pain of being removed from the vision of God. In the thirteenth century, however, Saint Thomas Aquinas (*c* 1225–74) took this one stage further, preaching that those in Limbo existed in a state of happiness and unity with God.

ABOVE: God and Satan; an illustration in the margin of an undated medieval illuminated manuscript. In his depiction of Satan – with his dragon-like fiery red wings, satyr-like haunches and the head of a lion (recalling the description of the beast of the Apocalypse as mentioned in Revelation 13:2) – the artist has created a hybrid, incorporating various of the iconographic attributes that had been used to denote Satan and his cohorts over the centuries. The Devil's mouth is open as if he is screaming, and his body is contorted as if in frustrated rage, but God looks down, unperturbed, his mouth closed in calm silence. In his left hand God holds an Orb, symbolising His sovereignty over all He surveys – Satan included.

OPPOSITE: Exorcising an *Oni*; an illustration from *Japan And Its Art* (1889). In Japanese folklore, *Oni* are demons; they are usually depicted as gigantic creatures, frequently with claws and two horns (this *Oni* has large, clawed hands and two small horns). Originally, *Oni* were benevolent in nature but over time they came to be strongly associated with evil. Today they are seen as bringers of bad luck and disaster and, at the annual *Setsubun* festivals that mark the last day of winter in Japan, householders throw beans out of the door while shouting 'Oni wa soto, Fuku wa Uchi' ('Demons [go] outside, Happiness [come] inside'); the ceremony is known as *mame-maki* (bean-throwing), *Oni harai* (devil-chasing) or *Tsuina* (evil-dispersing).

The Last Days

As seen elsewhere, it was in scenes of the Last Judgement – whether in
stained-glass, stone or wall paintings – that demons found their grisliest
representations. The Last Judgement is the Second Coming of Christ in
Christian doctrine, described in Matthew (25:31–46): 'When the Son of man
shall come in his glory . . . [and] as a shepherd divideth his sheep from the
goats: And he shall set the sheep on his right hand, but the goats on the left.'
(In the thirteenth century, some mystics believed that the year 1300 would
herald the Second Coming and the end of the world.) In such scenes, the dead
rise from their graves for the Final Judgement, then, the Judgement over, the
sheep (the good) are separated from the goats (the wicked) and conducted to
eternal reward or punishment. Just as angels bear away the souls of the
righteous to heaven, demons drive the souls of the damned into hell, and
often try to tip the scales of Saint Michael, weigher of souls, in an unfair bid
to claim another soul for the Devil.

It was taught that the Second Coming would unleash the Apocalypse as
detailed in Revelation, the last book of the Bible, whose author 'Saint John
the Divine' foretells the destruction of the wicked, the overthrow of Satan,
and the establishment of Christ's kingdom – the 'New Jerusalem' – on earth.
Amid the calamities that precede the final cataclysm the Antichrist is born
in Babylon, to form, with the Dragon and Beast from the Abyss, a Satanic
Trinity. Scenes of the Apocalypse abounded in medieval art (though in
sculpture, artists preferred to take their inspiration for end-time imagery
from Matthew's verses), famously disseminated through Dürer's series of 15
woodcuts. In such scenes Saint Michael may be depicted as slaying the
dragon (the passage in Revelation describing war in heaven also served as
the scriptural basis for the depiction of the Fall of the Rebel Angels, thereby
mingling past 'events' with a prophetic vision of the end of time), Satan
shown bound in chains, or the Four Horsemen of the Apocalypse sowing
death and destruction upon the opening of the first four seals.

In the unspecified time before the Last Judgement, however, one's own
death and judgement were urgent issues requiring preparation and, in this,
Ars Moriendi – the art of dying (well) – proved invaluable. Once the domain
of the clergy, from the fourteenth century such texts were illustrated and
used not just by priests attending the dying, but by laypeople as well. They
offered support for those in their last hours by helping the dying person to
affirm belief in their faith, in the hope of forgiveness, in patience and charity,
in humility, and to renounce earthly ties. The popularity of *Ars Moriendi*
marked a shift away from the concern with humanity's collective judgement
to the judgement that an individual would face immediately after death. An
illustrated *Ars Moriendi* would conclude with an idealised scene of a 'good
death', with an angel receiving the soul and demons writhing in frustration
at their defeat. The point was clearly made: believers must live a good life, or
face horrible punishment.

ABOVE: Stephan Lochner, *The Last Judgement, c* 1435. Christ the Judge, who is flanked by the Virgin Mary and Saint John the Evangelist – both kneeling intercessors – sits in judgement at the end of time, when the dead will rise from their graves and be consigned to an eternity in either paradise or hell. On the left, angels turn back those that are not of the elect who are trying to slip into paradise, and monstrous demons drag them away, beating and driving them into hell. Opposite the gates of paradise looms the city of Dis with its eternally burning towers and its gates patrolled by demons. In the centre foreground a demon pulls the fat body of a miser by the arm, who, pathetically, still clutches his bag of gold coins which scatter on the ground around him.

LEFT: *The Last Judgement* (1452) by Petrus Christus, in the Gemäldegalerie, Berlin, Germany. Instead of the saved and the damned being divided, left and right, and sent either rejoicing into the realm of the blessed, or wailing into the infernal regions of the doomed, a skeleton divides the dark netherworld from the verdant plain which extends to heaven, and from which the resurrected are rising from the earth. The elect, arrayed in heaven, look down on Saint Michael as he defeats the Devil in final battle, according to Revelation. Beneath the skeleton, tiny humans are pitched headlong into the flaming pit of hell, depicted as the gaping maws of Leviathan. As the conductor of souls to the other world and the devil's chief adversary, Saint Michael figures prominently in Last Judgement scenes.

LEFT: *The Four Horsemen of the Apocalypse*, a woodcut of 1498, from the series made by the German Renaissance artist Albrecht Dürer illustrating the vision of the Saint John as recounted by the 'beloved apostle' in the Book of Revelation. The artist compressed several verses into a single image that dramatically conveys the cataclysmic unleashing of the apocalyptic riders. The first rider, furthest away and carrying a bow, represents pestilence. The second, with a raised sword, has the power to unleash the calamity of war. The third, with empty scales flying behind him, represents famine. The fourth rider is Death, mounted on a skeletal-looking horse, sweeping all before him into the jaws of hell, the literally gaping mouth of the Leviathan-like creature, bottom left. Dürer's Apocalypse series, consisting of 15 woodcuts, revolutionized the art of the printed, illustrated book.

OPPOSITE: *The Woman Clothed with the Sun, and the Seven-Headed Dragon*, a woodcut by Albrecht Dürer from the Apocalypse series of woodcuts (1497–8) made to illustrate selected scenes from the Book of Revelation, which described the visions of Saint John on the isle of Patmos. This, the tenth woodcut in the series, illustrates Revelation 12:1, in which the 'wonder in heaven' – which appears after the seventh trumpet has sounded – takes the shape of 'a woman clothed with the sun, and the moon under her feet, and upon her head a crown of twelve stars', interpreted as the Virgin. The fiery dragon, 'having seven heads and ten horns, and seven crowns upon his heads', represents Satan, who went to make war with 'the remnant of her seed' – it stood waiting to devour the child she is about to bear, who here is swept up to heaven by angels.

LEFT: A detail from a woodcut by the German Renaissance artist Albrecht Dürer depicting *The Angel with the Key to the Bottomless Pit*, as described in the Book of Revelation: 'And I saw an angel come down from heaven, having the key of the bottomless pit and a great chain in his hand; And he laid hold on the dragon, that old serpent, which is the Devil, and Satan, and bound him a thousand years' (Revelation 20:3). The act of 'binding', or incarcerating, Satan meant limiting his power on earth; for according to the Bible, Christ's sacrifice on the Cross had destroyed 'him that had the power of death, that is, the devil' (Hebrews 2:14). This woodcut was the last in the series of 15 made by the artist in 1497 and 1498 to illustrate selected scenes from the Revelation of Saint John.

OPPOSITE: A painted miniature from the *Commentary to the Apocalypse* by the Beatus of Liébana, an early medieval illuminated manuscript produced in the monastery of Santo Domingo de Silos, near Burgos, Spain. Also known as the Silos Apocalypse, it was completed in 1109 and illustrated by an illuminator named Petrus. This jewel-like page depicts the Four Horsemen of the Apocalypse, from the Book of Revelation. The Four Horsemen appear in Revelation 6:1–8, in which Saint John describes the opening of the first four seals. The first rider, top left, holding a bow, is the 'conqueror'; the second, top right, wielding a sword, signifies 'war'; the third, carrying an empty pair of scales, is 'famine'; the fourth, on a 'pale horse', is 'Death' – here, accompanied by a black, winged demon.

ABOVE: The host of Satan; an illustration from the *Douce Apocalypse*. One of the finest of the great number of Apocalypse manuscripts produced during the thirteenth century, the *Douce Apocalypse* was created for Edward, son of the English King Henry III, between about 1250 and 1270; a few of the illustrations were never completed. This scene illustrates Revelation 20:8, in which Satan – loosed from his prison after 1,000 years (shown left) – gathers his armies to lead (right) a final assault on the Church and all Christians. Satan's soldiers are armed and dressed in contemporary style, perhaps more effectively to relate the story to the experience and knowledge of readers of the time. The illustrator, however, emphasizes that this is not some courtly army bent on a chivalrous mission: for the leader's satyr-like lower half is naked (no courtly armour for him) and his shield and standard (behind Satan, right) clearly display his 'arms' – three toads, symbols of death, lust and carnality.

ABOVE: A twelfth-century Venetian ivory, now in the Victoria and Albert Museum, London, depicting the Last Judgement scene. It is divided horizontally into three sections with, vertically, the left and right parts of the composition balancing one another in careful symmetry, although they convey diametrically opposing messages: the one, left, being a joyful message of eternal life; the other, right, speaking of eternal damnation and despair. In the top tier sits Christ the Judge, flanked by the twelve apostles, with, nearest to him, the Virgin Mary and John the Baptist – rays of hope, as intercessors, in even the most solemn circumstances of justice. Seraphim, first among the angelic choirs, hover beneath the heavenly throne. The dead, in the second tier, have risen from their tombs and now appear before their Judge; those who are damned before the tribunal, right, are chased into hell by an angel. There, Satan – in a human guise – sits on a throne of devouring serpents, with a tiny, naked Antichrist on his lap. As a holy counterpoint, in heaven (bottom left) the patriarch Abraham, seated on his throne, bears in his bosom the souls of the righteous.

OPPOSITE: An allegorical depiction of the 'Hour of Death', from a fifteenth-century *Liber Horarum* (Book of Hours), where it prefaced a Service for the Dead. The sinner, at the point of death, is shown faced with all his sins; he turns away from them to listen – too late – to the advice of his good angel. His conscience, black with all his faults, reminds him of them all, and remorse, like a serpent, devours his heart. The dying man is suspended between hell, the literally gaping mouth of a Leviathan-like sea creature, spewing flames, and God in heaven, who holds the sword of justice in his right hand. Death, holding a spear, stands behind him ready to strike, and a taloned but otherwise anthropomorphic demon stands by, ready to claim another soul for the hell fires.

ABOVE: Detail from the twelfth-century fresco depicting the Doom, or the Last Judgement, in the church at Chaldon, Surrey, England. The ladder visible here represents the Ladder of Salvation, the top part of which is attended by angels, and the lower part populated by devils which are torturing the damned in hell. Doomsday was a popular subject for church wall-paintings in medieval times, and the Doom was usually set over the chancel arch, where it dominated the parochial congregation; beyond, the chancel itself was the priest's domain. For the medieval parishioners, the term 'Doom' would not in itself have implied damnation; rather, it referred to the 'time of trial', during which the fate of an individual's soul was sealed.

ABOVE: An angel with the key to the abyss is shown 'binding' Satan in this seventeenth-century engraving of a scene from Revelation. In chapter 20 of the Book of Revelation (20:1–3), towards the final chapter of the visions of Saint John, an angel with the key of hell and a chain seizes the dragon, 'that serpent of old', chains him and throws him into a pit for a thousand years. The chaining of Satan for a thousand years symbolized Christ's victory, through His resurrection, over death and the forces of evil; the time span was not meant to be taken literally, and, instead, was meant to symbolize the long period of time between the limiting of Satan's power and the end of the world. The implication being that during this time, God's people could share in His heavenly glory, after death, by virtue of the Christian victory over death and sin.

ABOVE: The Dragon Fighting with the Servants of God; a panel from the *Angers Apocalypse*. Commissioned by Louis, Duc d'Anjou, the *Angers Apocalypse* – a great tapestry woven between 1375 and 1382 to decorate the Great Hall of the Château of Angers, France – depicts scenes from Revelation. After the dragon – Satan – has been cast out of Heaven to earth by Saint Michael in Revelation 12:7–9, it 'persecuted the woman which brought forth the man child'. The woman escapes on two great Eagle's wings (12:14). The dragon then pours forth a great river in an attempt to trap her, but the Earth 'swallowed' it up. In this scene, 'wroth with the woman', the dragon makes war with the 'remnant' of the woman's offspring 'which keep the commandments of God, and have the testimony of Jesus Christ' (Revelation 12:17). It is probable that the author of Revelation intended the woman to be a symbol of the Church, but the medieval theologian Saint Bonaventure (c 1217–74) and others identified her with Mary.

ABOVE: This scene from the *Angers Apocalypse* tapestries illustrates Revelation 13, in which John of Patmos (who is depicted on the left), author of the Book, reports his vision that Satan, the dragon with seven heads (right), will pass his power to the Beast from the Sea – the Antichrist (centre): 'And they worshipped the dragon, which gave power unto the beast: and they worshipped the beast … And all that dwell upon the earth shall worship him, whose names are not written in the book of life of the Lamb slain from the foundation of the world'(13:4, 8). This panel is of particular interest in showing clearly how the Apocalypse story was used to comment on fourteenth-century politics. Firstly, although the Antichrist is depicted as a beast, it has the symbols of temporal power: it sits on a throne-cushion; it looks, autocratically, directly at the observer; and it holds a symbol of French power, a sceptre tipped with the fleur-de-lis. In short, the viewer is encouraged to view the Antichrist as a monstrous, contemporary king, supported by Satan (who is here, literally, the power behind the throne). Given that the English invaders had gained possession of Aquitaine in 1356, French viewers would have recognized that this monstrous, Satanic king was intended to be none other than the English monarch, Edward III (1312–77), under whom the Hundred Years' War had begun between France and England in 1337.

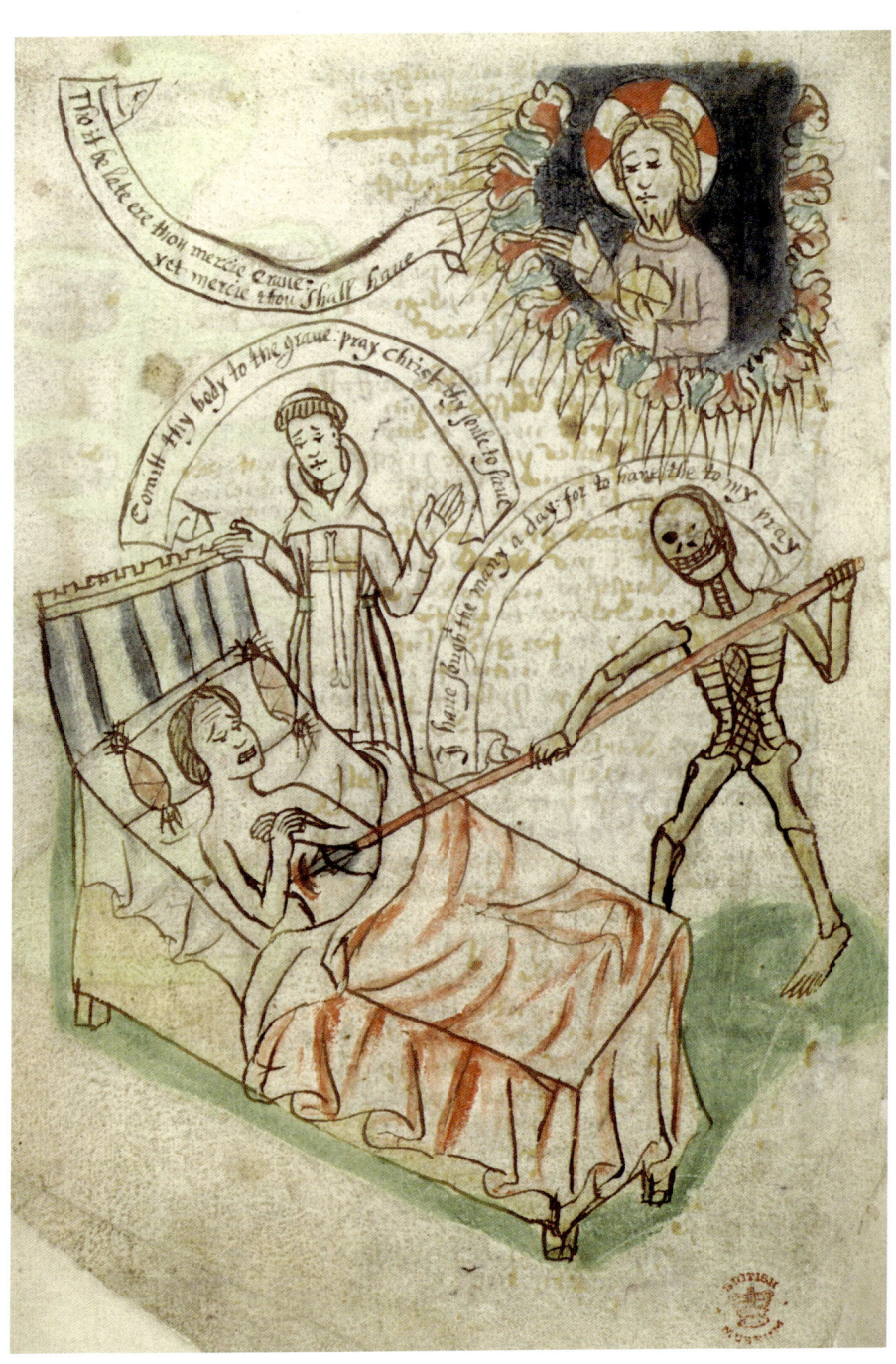

OPPOSITE: In this English illustration from the late Middle Ages, a plague victim receives the last rites from a priest, while the smiling figure of death – drawn as a skeleton – pierces the dying man with a lance. The banderol above the priest reads: 'Commit thy body to the grave; pray Christ thy soul to save.' Such images of mortality became far more common, and much more explicit in their depictions of death, after the arrival of the Black Death in Europe in 1348 – a grim reaper, indeed, decimating its population. They were commonly found in books known as *ars moriendi* – the art of dying. In such works, both author and image-maker stressed the final moments of life, when it still hung in the balance whether, by prayer, faith and repentance, a person might prove himself worthy of salvation. In this scene, Christ looks down, the banner next to him indicating that this dying soul can look forward to a heavenly reward: 'Though it be late […] yet mercy thou shall have'.

ABOVE: *Saint Francis Borgia at the Deathbed of an Impenitent*, 1788, by the Spanish painter Francisco Goya. The sixteenth-century Spanish saint Francis Borgia was of noble ancestry but became a protector of the Jesuits and one of their number; in this painting he is shown in simple Jesuit attire. The dying man's sufferings are acutely apparent, and are compounded by the presence of the demonic creatures hovering by his side, infernal flames flickering around them. While some see the painting as a portrayal of exorcism, a more plausible interpretation (put forward by Frank Heckes) is that this is a scene of damnation, its source an eighteenth-century life of the saint by Cardinal Alvaro Cienfuego. That text recounted that the figure of Christ on the Crucifix held by Saint Francis hurled a fistful of blood at the impenitent man, whose soul was consigned to fiery and frightful demons.

OPPOSITE: An engraving depicting *A Knight, Death and the Devil* by the Northern Renaissance artist Albrecht Dürer, made in 1513. The knight represents the Christian soldier (Dürer's contemporary, Erasmus had written a *Handbook of the Christian Soldier* in 1501). He gazes straight ahead, ignoring the figure of Death who is mounted on an old nag. Wrapped about by snakes, Death holds up an hourglass, symbol of the unstoppable march of time. The Devil is depicted as a horned beast with cloven feet and the snout of a boar; although he carries a menacing-looking pike, he is distinctly less powerful than the knight, whose unflinching resolve is underpinned by his faith (also personified by the dog which accompanies him). The city in the background – possibly the Heavenly Jerusalem – would appear to be his ultimate destination.

ABOVE: A painted miniature from the fifteenth-century *Savoyard Apocalypse*, depicting the Harlot with the kings of the earth, an episode from Revelation, chapter 17. The Harlot personifies the city of Babylon, the antithesis of the New Jerusalem. She is seated upon a beast with seven heads and ten horns with, around her neck, a gold chain signifying royal status; her red hair is loose about her shoulders and her tight-fitting robe cut low at the breast and of rich gilded fabric. She is accompanied by the kings of the earth, who fondle her and covet her. The Harlot is the Devil's instrument, one of the satanic powers sent out to ensnare those in authority to encourage them to take up arms against God in the final conflict.

ABOVE: Satan loosed from prison; an illustration from a thirteenth-century illuminated manuscript. In Revelation (20:1-3) the angel shuts Satan in prison for 1,000 years but the narrator warns that 'after that he must be loosed a little season'. Here, Satan is being freed from his 'prison' to go out for one last time 'to deceive the nations which are in the four quarters of the earth, Gog and Magog' (20:8). After this brief resurgence, Satan and evil experience their final, and complete destruction ('And death and hell were cast into the lake of fire. This is the second death' (20:14)), which heralds the Second Coming.

OPPOSITE: Death, depicted as a skeleton figure wielding a scythe, is shown riding a funereal carriage studded with human skulls and bones and drawn by four black oxen with rings through their noses. In depictions such as this one, Death was not simply a *memento mori* (a reminder to mortals of the inescapable moment when their lives on earth would end) but an advancing, crushing chariot destroying all, including kings, courtiers and cardinals, in its path – for this was Death, the great leveller. In the top left corner angels fly towards the heavenly light with the souls of the saved, while, top right, demons make off with the damned, fleeing into a rain of fire. They reminded the viewer of the ineluctability of the end of time – and the certainty of an afterlife spent either in heaven or hell.

LEFT: A sculptural detail from the Last Judgement carved tympanum on the twelfth-century Cathedral of Saint-Lazare in Autun (Saône-et-Loire), France. This part of the relief (c 1130–40) shows the battle between an angel and demons during the psychostasis, or 'weighing of souls', which is conducted by Saint Michael at the final judgement. Here, the struggle is active and patently physical, with gleeful, shrieking demons trying unfairly to tip the scales and claim another soul for Satan. The depiction of the demons is startling; their striated muscles and ribs are visible, as though they have been flayed, and their open mouths reveal teeth. The demon on the right holds a toad, while the one gripping the scales has a three-headed snake wrapped about his calves. The contrast between their violent, erratic movements, and the graceful calm of the angel could hardly be greater. Unusually, the carved relief – located in the tympanum over the west (main) portal – was signed, in stone, by 'Gislebertus'.

OPPOSITE: A detail of the tympanum on the façade of the basilica of Sainte-Madeleine, Vézelay (Yonne), France depicting the Risen Christ surrounded by apostles, with – in the lintel and innermost arch – all the peoples of the earth who have heard His message. Christ is here the teacher, rather than the final judge, with the sculptural group conflating biblical descriptions of the Ascension, Pentecost (the rays of light from Christ's hand signify the descent of the Holy Ghost) and the Mission of the Apostles (Acts 1:4–9). It would have served as a sermon for pilgrims and crusaders who flocked to Vézelay in the Middle Ages (it was from Vézelay that Richard the Lionheart and King Philip of France set out on the Third Crusade), and reinforced the teaching that Christ came to preach the Gospel to the whole human race, and that the Church should carry the message to the ends of the Earth.

ABOVE: A sculptural detail from the Last Judgement carved relief in the tympanum of the thirteenth-century Cathedral of Saint-Étienne in Bourges (Cher), France. The tympanum – regarded by many as the finest sculptural group of the Last Judgement scene – is located on the west (main) portal of the cathedral. Saint Michael the warrior archangel here becomes a smiling angel in graceful robes. Michael places a protective arm around one of the naked youths who have been raised from the dead; this fortunate individual will join the ranks of the elect, filing off to the archangel's right. To the right of the saint – and starkly contrasted – is the Devil; he is naked, leering and has bestial features (a goatish, Pan-like head and a clearly visible penis). The demon immediately to the right of the Devil has a gaping, rictus grin, a second face on his abdomen and an arm forming a second appendage.

ABOVE: In this altarpiece (c 1435–40) by Fra Angelico, now in Berlin, the dead have risen from their tombs following the resurrection of the flesh, which, according to the Bible, will take place after the Second Coming of Christ at the end of time. Angels are shown carrying the trumpets of the Last Judgement, which they have sounded (Matthew 24:31) – the open tombs equally indicating that bodily resurrection has already taken place. Below the Risen Christ (enthroned, and flanked in heaven by angels and the ranks of the elect), the living and the dead are judged, then to be consigned – in the light of their deeds – to heaven or hell, according to the Gospel of Saint Matthew (25:31–34). In this book of the New Testament, the apostle relates Christ's discourse to his disciples: 'And before him [Christ the Judge] shall be gathered all nations: and he shall separate them one from another, as a shepherd divideth his sheep from the goats'.

OPPOSITE: This medieval illustration depicts the Fourth Horseman of the Apocalypse, referred to in Revelation (6:8). The fourth horseman is Death itself – here, a sword-wielding skeleton – who is closely followed, according to the Book of Revelation, by hell, here a gaping-jawed Leviathan breathing fire and swallowing up all from the highest to the lowest ranks of man. Above is a lamb, described in Revelation (5:6–14) as having seven horns and seven eyes. The lamb carries a scroll, shown here, on which is inscribed the secrets of man's destiny; it is kept shut by seven seals. Hanging beneath the scroll in this illustration are the first four seals – now open, and thereby unleashing the Four Horsemen of the Apocalypse.

Animal quartum· ven̄ ꝑ vide·

OPPOSITE: A woodcut illustration from an *Ars Moriendi* (*The Art of Dying*) of *c* 1500, showing the demons and angels attendant at the deathbed, with Christ as supreme Lord. A popular consolatory manual, by 1500 the *Ars Moriendi* was a widely disseminated genre within the large body of 'death literature', being circulated in particular via 'block books', whose pictures and text were printed from carved blocks of wood. There were two versions of *Ars moriendi* – the first was a treatise of six chapters, with prayers and rites for use at the hour of death, while the second was the shorter and more popular version, showing the dying person's struggle with temptations before attaining a 'good death'. Common to both was the treatment of the deathbed scene as a narrative, culminating in the – presumably – successful navigation of the maze of doubt and temptation. In this woodcut, demons tempt the dying man with crowns, symbols of pride; other 'temptations' shown to beset the dying person included despair and a lack of faith.

ABOVE: An illustration from a medieval translation of Saint Augustine's *The City of God*, by the French magistrate Raoul de Presles (*c* 1270–1330). Augustine, one of the Church Fathers, began writing this work in 410, in the fallout from the Sack of Rome – for which many pagans blamed the Empire's conversion to Christianity. In his book, Augustine traced the history of two cities – the Earthly and the Heavenly – from the beginning of time. This scene shows Saint Michael – the chief actor, after Christ, in scenes of the Last Judgement – weighing the souls of the dead in an elaborate pair of scales. Such iconography did not originate in the gospels, but was founded in a metaphor almost as old as humanity – that of virtues and vices hanging in the balance at the judgement of the dead. (In ancient Egypt, for example, the hearts of the dead were weighed, according to the *Book of the Dead*, in a ritual supervized by Anubis and Horus.) Later, in the West, the Church Fathers applied the metaphor freely, with Augustine writing of 'good and evil actions [being as if] hanging in the scales, and if the evil preponderate the guilty shall be dragged to hell'.

ABOVE: An illustration from an English Apocalypse manuscript from the late thirteenth century, showing the Beast from the Earth and the Beast from the Sea – both the Devil's cohorts in the Book of Revelation. The Beast from the Sea is shown with seven heads and ten horns, each crowned by a diadem, according to Revelation 13; it was intended by its author to be identified with the Antichrist, the great deceiver. Here, the Beast of the Earth, left, emerges from the abyss; this beast lures people to worship the Beast from the Sea. Men are shown prostrating themselves before it; they are forced to worship it on pain of death and receive the mark of the devil on their right hand and forehead before they can traffic in earthly goods. In Revelation there ensues the chain of events which constitute the harvest of the world at the time of Judgement.

OPPOSITE (ABOVE): A woodcut illustration of a scene from Daniel, a book in both the Old Testament and the Hebrew Bible. The second part of the book (chapters 7–12) describes the visions of the Hebrew prophet. One such vision was of four beasts rising up from the sea; each fantastic creature is taken to represent an earthly kingdom – thus a lion with eagle's wings (Babylon), a bear (Persia), a leopard with four wings like a bird (Greece), and a terrible beast with ten horns, which later become eight horns (Rome). The latter was a prefiguration of the first beast of Revelation – the Beast from the Sea – and it, likewise, tramples over the earth, its ten horns representing ten kings. In his visionary depiction of the Second Coming, John of Patmos (also known as John the Divine), author of Revelation – written towards the end of the first century AD – was inspired by Daniel, who was writing in the second century BC, and other Jewish Apocalyptic literature.

LEFT: This painted miniature from an Apocalypse manuscript of the Middle Ages illustrates a verse from chapter 16 of Revelation: 'And I saw three unclean spirits like frogs come out of the mouth of the dragon, and out of the mouth of the beast, and out of the mouth of the false prophet' (16:13). The seven-headed Beast from the Sea, with its source in Revelation 13, was the Antichrist, and was understood to be such by the manuscript's owner. The dragon, 'that old serpent', was equally identifiable as Satan. The False Prophet was understood to be the Beast from the Earth; here, he is shown as a man like Christ, and in this guise presents a most insidious danger. In Revelation the three satanic powers form an unholy Satanic trinity, in emulation of – and in opposition to – the Christian trinity of Father, Son and Holy Ghost.

OPPOSITE: An engraving from the 1688 folio edition of John Milton's *Paradise Lost*, the first illustrated edition of the epic poem. Set in its frontispiece was an engraved portrait of the poet by Robert White, while most of the engravings inside the book, from illustrations by different hands, were made by Michael Burgesse. This plate depicts verses from Book Two, in which Satan encounters Sin and Death at the gates of hell. Sin is Satan's daughter, while Death (carrying a 'dreadful dart') is both his son and grandson – the offspring of his incestuous union with Sin. Sin is shown, following Milton's verses, as beautiful from the waist up but a hideous serpent beneath, and surrounded by hellhounds (the product of a further incestuous liaison with Death, her son) that move in and out of her womb. Death, meanwhile, is a ghastly, shadowy spectre – 'fierce as ten furies, terrible as hell'. At judgement day, Death and Sin will both be sealed in hell, with Satan.

ABOVE: An illustration from a fourteenth-century illuminated manuscript on the Apocalypse, here depicting the Beast from the Sea and the dragon. Based on verses from Revelation (13:1–10), a beast with seven heads and ten horns, left, rises up from the sea; on the right, a multi-headed dragon rears up. The Beast from the Sea represents the Devil on earth; as the Antichrist, it speaks out against God and the faithful. The dragon – Satan – gives this beast its power. Its authority is buttressed in subsequent verses by the appearance of another beast – a beast coming up out of the earth, with 'two horns like a lamb' and with the voice of a dragon (13:11). This Beast from the Earth seduces people to worship the image of the Beast from the Sea by the lure of false miracles. The next chapter (14) describes this demonic threat countered by a vision of the Lamb on Mount Sion, in the company of the redeemed.

ABOVE: An illustration from the *Sutra of the Ten Kings*, a painting on paper roll. This incomplete roll, part of an apocryphal *sutra* dated AD 903, shows two of the Ten Kings of Hell. The Ten Kings preside over the successive spheres through which a soul must pass on its way to rebirth. After death, the soul comes before the first seven kings at seven-day intervals, before the eighth king on the hundredth day, the ninth on the first anniversary of death, and, finally, the tenth on the third anniversary. The kings illustrate the Buddhist concept of judgement after death in its most fully developed form. Here, two kings sit before a draped table attended by the Good and Bad Boys (recorders of a person's good and evil deeds during life). A virtuous couple, carrying *sutra* rolls and an image of the Buddha, contrast with sinners in chains and *cangues* being driven past by their bull-headed jailers. The breaks in the scroll are before and after this next scene. A last king is shown with the six *Gati* ('Ways of Rebirth'), each represented by trailing clouds. Depicted in descending order, these are the Ways of divine beings, titanic demons, men, animals, hungry ghosts and hell. The final dramatic scene shows figures running from a flaming city of hell towards the *bodhisattva* Kshitigarbha, who has the power to save souls from the evil forms of rebirth. The rolls were found in a cave in Gansu province, China, and today are held at the British Museum, London.

OPPOSITE: A fresco of the Last Judgement scene by Giotto di Bondone; it is in the Arena Chapel (also known as the Scrovegni chapel, after its founding family) in Padua, Italy. Covering the west wall, the scene formed part of an elaborate cycle of frescos executed by Giotto between 1303 and 1305. In the middle, Christ the Judge sits enthroned and surrounded by burning seraphim. The twelve apostles are seated, left and right, as Christ foretold in Matthew (19:28): 'Ye shall be seated on twelve thrones and judge the twelve tribes of Israel.' Above them are throngs of angels. Beneath the figure of Christ is the Cross, reminding the fourteenth-century viewer that He was crucified for them – and justifying His anger that, although He died to saved them, not all men were willing to profit by that sacrifice, and thus will find themselves consigned to eternal hell – here, presided over by a monstrous, bloated and charred-looking Satan, on whom, with his cohort of dark demons, rain the fires of damnation. Significantly, the fresco is located over the door by which the congregation would leave – and in the minds of the faithful, passing through, the scene above their heads might at any moment become a reality.

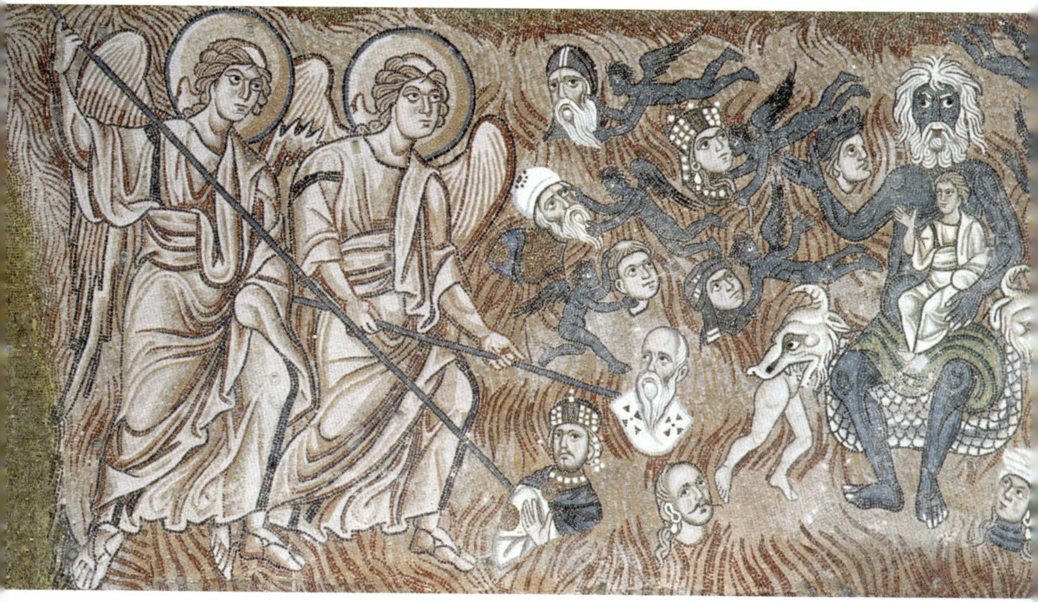

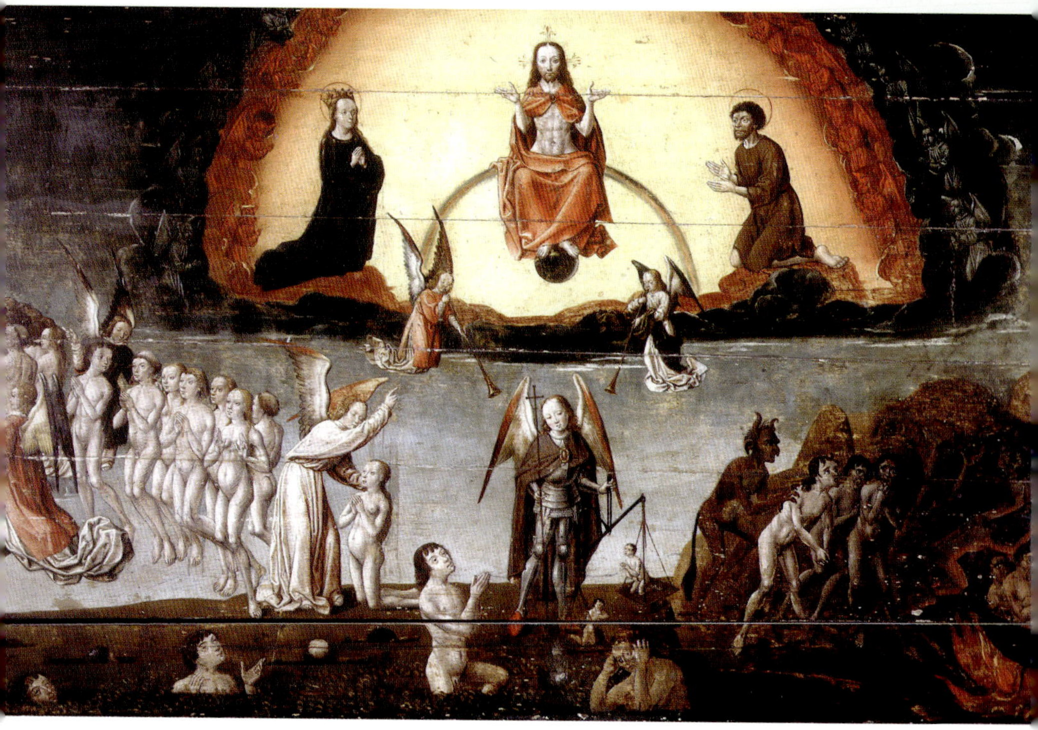

OPPOSITE (ABOVE): Detail of the twelfth-century mosaic decoration on the west wall of the church of Santa Maria Assunta on the island of Torcello, near Venice, Italy. Depicting the Last Judgement, it shows the damned being pitched into the hell, where small black demons inflict torments on them. Presiding over hell is Satan, drawn with human features, although as dark as his infernal cohorts. On Satan's lap sits the Antichrist who, in the Book of Revelation, is described as a hideous beast. Here, however, he is simply a man, reflecting the iconography that grew out of the writings of saints Augustine and Ambrose.

OPPOSITE (BELOW): A fifteenth-century painted panel depicting the Last Judgement scene, painted on wood by an unknown artist at the Priory of Orchaise, near Blois, in the Loire region of France. Christ sits in judgement as the resurrected rise from their graves. Saint Michael – cloaked in armour, as befits his role as chief adversary of the devil and as protecting saint of the Church Militant – performs the task of weighing the souls. Throughout the Middle Ages, Michael was held to be the conductor of souls (rather in the manner of Mercury, the pagan guide of the dead in classical times). Here, the righteous soul is the heavier of the two being weighed, and it tips the pan on the right side of Christ – the side of justice – from where the blessed are transported up to heaven. A demon, meanwhile, propels the damned into the fires of hell, right.

ABOVE: This engraving illustrates a scene from chapter nine of the Book of Revelation (9:1–11), in which the sounding of the fifth trumpet by an angel causes a star to fall into the abyss. This in turn unlooses a plague of monstrous locusts from the pit, which are led by their demonic king Abaddon; the locust army, as shown here, have human heads and sting with their tails, which terminate in scorpion heads. The locust army kills a third of humankind – all those not of the multitude of Christians who have received the protective 'seal' of the 'living God' on their foreheads, as described in an earlier chapter in Revelation (7:1–8). Revelation speaks of seven angel trumpeters; as each trumpet sounds, a calamity falls on the earth.

INDEX

Figures in italics indicate picture captions.

PICTURE CREDITS

The publishers would like to thank the following sources for their kind permission to reproduce the photographs in this book.

Key: t=Top, b=Bottom, c=Centre, l=Left and r=Right

akg-images: 39t, 43, 138–9, 148, 205, 209, 223; /Orsi Battaglini: 152, 153; /British Library: 31; /Camerapress: 2–3, 71, 93, 251, 252t; /Stefan Diller: 208; /Rabatti-Dominige: 121, 200; /Jean-Paul Dumontier: 27, 193; /Erich Lessing: 1, 128–9, 168, 180, 203; /Nimatallah: 142

Ancient Art & Architecture Collection: /R.Sheridan: 89, 92, 145

Bodleian Library, University of Oxford: 227

The Bridgeman Art Library: /Ahura Mazda triumphing over Angra Mainyu, copy of a frieze from Persepolis (colour litho), French School, (19th century)/ Bibliotheque des Arts Decoratifs, Paris, France, Archives Charmet: 7; /Every Dog has his Day, or Black Devils Amusing Themselves with a White Negro Driver, 1818 (colour litho), Cruikshank, George (1792–1878)/Private Collection: 4–5; /The Fall of the Rebel Angels, 1562 (oil on panel), Brueghel, Pieter the Elder (c1515–69)/Musees Royaux des Beaux-Arts de Belgique, Brussels, Belgium, Giraudon: 184–5; /The Garden of Earthly Delights, Hell, right wing of triptych,c 1500 (oil on panel), Bosch, Hieronymus (c1450–1516)/Prado, Madrid, Spain: 149; /The Haywain: right wing of the triptych depicting Hell,c 1500 (panel), Bosch, Hieronymus (c1450–1516)/Monasterio de El Escorial, Spain: 61; /The Heavy Stone, detail from the Life of St Benedict (c480–c550), in the Sacristy, 1387 (fresco), Spinello or Spinelli, Aretino Luca (c1340–1410)/San Miniato al Monte, Florence, Italy: 18; /Hell, right hand panel from the Triptych of Earthly Vanity and Divine Salvation,c 1485 (oil on panel), Memling, Hans (c 1433–94)/Musee des Beaux-Arts, Strasbourg, France, Giraudon: 10; /'Hell Broke Loose, or the Murder of Louis', 1793 (coloured engraving), Dent, W. (fl.1793–1847)/Musee de la Revolution Francaise, Vizille, France: 11; /The Inferno, detail of a man being violated by a fantastical creature (oil on panel), Bles, Herri met de (Civetta) (c 1510-p.1550)/Palazzo Ducale, Venice, Italy, Cameraphoto Arte Venezia: 65; /Last Judgement: detail from the bottom right corner, Sistine Chapel (fresco), Buonarroti, Michelangelo (1475–1564)/Vatican Museums and Galleries, Vatican City, Italy: 130; /The Last Judgement, detail of Satan devouring the damned in hell, c 1431 (oil on panel), Angelico, Fra (Guido di Pietro) (c 1387–1455)/Museo di San Marco dell'Angelico, Florence, Italy, Giraudon: 40–41; /The Nightmare, 1781 (oil on canvas), Fuseli, Henry (Fussli, Johann Heinrich) (1741–1825)/The Detroit Institute of Arts, USA, Founders Society purchase with Mr and Mrs Bert L. Smokler: 32–33; /St Bernard of Menthon (923–1008) Overcoming a Demon, from a Book of Hours, 1490 (vellum), French School, (15th century)/Bibliotheque de l'Arsenal, Paris, France, Archives Charmet: 187; St Francis Borgia (1510–72) Helping a Dying Impenitent, 1795 (oil on canvas), /Goya y Lucientes, Francisco Jose de (1746–1828) / Valencia Cathedral, Valencia, Spain: 235; /St George and the Dragon, c 1439–40 (tempera on panel) (for detail see 85552), Uccello, Paolo (1397–1475)/Musee Jacquemart-Andre, Paris, France: 214; /St George and the

Dragon, c 1470 (oil on canvas) (for detail see 85548), Uccello, Paolo (1397–1475)/ National Gallery, London, UK: 215; /St Michael, c 1503–05 (oil on panel) Raphael (Raffaello Sanzio of Urbino) (1483–1520)/Louvre, Paris, France, Giraudon: 8; /St Michael Killing the Dragon (oil on panel), Lieferinxe, Josse (Master of St Sebastian) (fl.1493–1508)/Musee du Petit Palais, Avignon, France: 176; /St Philip Exorcising a Demon, c 1497–1500 (fresco), Lippi, Filippino (c 1457–1504)/Santa Maria Novella, Florence, Italy: 190

©The British Library: 182

Corbis: /©The Art Archive: 206; /©Arte & Immagini srl: 25; /©Bettmann: 107; /©Christie's Images: 48–9, 78; /©Fine Art Photographic Library: 20; /©David Lees: 167b; /©Massimo Listri: 110; /©Araldo de Luca: 171b; /©Sandro Vannini: 12–13, 21, 22

Mary Evans Picture Library: 106

Photos12.com: /ARJ: 30, 150, 222, 232, 233; /Anne Joudiou: 131b; /Oasis: 70; /Oronoz: 237

Picture Desk/The Art Archive: /Bodleian Library Oxford: 154; /Museo del Prado Madrid: 60, 62–3, 100–101; /Palazzo Pubblico Siena/Dagli Orti: 112

RMN: /©Jean-Gilles Berizzi: 45t; /©Gérard Blot: 201

Tate, London: 135, 164

Topfoto.co.uk: 15, 19b, 23, 24, 26t&b, 35, 36, 37, 59, 64, 72, 74, 76b, 86, 87, 94, 115, 126, 131t, 137t&b, 146t&b, 151b, 156, 163, 166, 167t, 170, 172–173, 177, 178t&b, 179, 181, 186, 194, 196–197, 213, 216, 218, 228, 229, 238, 242, 243, 246, 247t&b; /©Ann Ronan Picture Library: 183; /AM Media/HIP: 16, 79; /©The British Museum/HIP: 14, 19t, 28, 47, 55, 73, 76t, 77, 80–81, 82, 83, 85t, 95t, 96, 97, 99, 102, 103t, 105, 114, 118, 120, 125, 140, 141, 155, 162, 192, 199, 212, 220–21, 224t, 226, 234, 236, 239, 248, 249, 250; /City of London: 45b; /EE Images/HIP: 42; /©Fortean: 44, 58t&b, 85b, 90–91, 101, 109, 111, 123, 124t&b, 157b, 158, 171t, 198, 207, 210–11, 219, 224b, 225, 231, 253; /Fotomas: 98t&b; /HIP: 147; /©Larry Mangino/ The Image Works: 38; /©Ray Roberts: 240b; /©Roger-Viollet: 17, 52, 104, 136, 143, 151t, 169, 174, 175, 204, 217, 240t, 241, 245, 252b; /©Charles Walker: 29, 34, 39b, 46, 50, 53, 54, 56, 57, 66, 67t&b, 68, 69, 75, 84, 88, 103b, 108, 113, 116, 117t&b, 118, 122, 133, 134, 144, 157t, 159, 160–161, 165, 188, 189, 191, 195, 202, 230, 244; /©Woodmansterne: 95b

V&A Images: 50–51

Every effort has been made to acknowledge correctly and contact the source and/or copyright holder of each picture and Carlton Books Limited apologizes for any unintentional errors or omissions, which will be corrected in future editions of this book.